GIVE ME LIBERTY

GIVE ME LIBERTY

VIRGINIA & THE FORGING OF A NATION

Essays by

Antonio T. Bly, Woody Holton, Sarah E. McCartney, Alan Taylor, Karin Wulf

VIRGINIA MUSEUM OF HISTORY & CULTURE

Virginia Museum of History & Culture in association with D Giles Limited

INIA

Give Me Liberty: Virginia & The Forging of a Nation celebrates the exhibition at the Virginia Museum of History & Culture, March 22, 2025–January 4, 2026, and at the American Revolution Museum at Yorktown, Virginia, July 1, 2026–January 31, 2027.

First published jointly in 2025 by GILES
An imprint of D Giles Limited
66 High Street,
Lewes, BN7 1XG, UK
gilesltd.com

EU GPSR Authorised Representative
LOGOS EUROPE, 9 rue Nicolas Poussin,
17000, LA ROCHELLE, France
E-mail: Contact@logoseurope.eu

ISBN: 978-1-913875-58-9

Images in this book from the collection of the Virginia Museum of History & Culture are credited as VMHC.

For D Giles Limited:
Copy-edited and proof-read by Jenny Wilson
Designed by Alfonso Iacurci
Produced by GILES, an imprint of D Giles Limited
Printed and bound in Europe

Front cover: *Patrick Henry Before the Virginia House of Burgesses* (detail), Peter F. Rothermel, 1851, oil on canvas. Collection of the Patrick Henry Memorial Foundation
Back cover: *Surrender of Cornwallis*, John Trumbull, 1914, print. Library of Congress
Frontispiece: *Patrick Henry* (detail), Thomas Sully, 1851, oil on canvas. VMHC, Gift of Thomas Sully
Pp. 4–5: *Patrick Henry Arguing the Parson's Cause at Hanover Courthouse* (detail), George Cooke, about 1830, oil on canvas. VMHC

MIX
Paper | Supporting responsible forestry
FSC® C118234
FSC www.fsc.org

Contents

Foreword

Growing up in Williamsburg, Virginia, history was all around me. Home to the largest living history museum in the world, it was once the capital city of the biggest, wealthiest, and most diverse North American English colony on the eve of the American Revolution. "Give Me Liberty" along with "All Men are Created Equal" was recited regularly—especially during Fourth of July celebrations. None were bigger than the Bicentennial, which forever changed our community. Visitors from around the world descended on Virginia's Historic Triangle (Jamestown/Williamsburg/Yorktown) to revel in the traditional narrative of American democracy and enjoy patriotic experiences, food, and fireworks.

Within a few hours' drive of the Historic Triangle, plantations belonging to "Founding Fathers" Patrick Henry, Thomas Jefferson, James Monroe, George Mason, James Madison, and George Washington were also easily accessible. Visitors flocked to these historic sites too, each one rich with stories of genteel patriots revolting against unfair taxes while dutiful "servants" and wives kept the home fires burning. These common depictions of the Revolutionary era suggested the United States was only shaped by affluent, European-descended men and their families who in fact represented less than 20 percent of the population. For decades, the impression was that they alone created a great nation out of a vast, empty wilderness.

Visitors marveled at how things "back then" were made, how people dressed, the types of foods grown, the goods consumed, and how people defended themselves. Rarely was consideration given to who produced and labored to make these environments possible. Nowhere could a visitor see how more than 80 percent of the eighteenth-century American population lived and worked. Despite not being able to vote or hold public offices, the majority—women and men of various backgrounds and social stations—influenced political thinking by their actions, words, and presence. They forced changes that have become a hallmark of American life—the right to peaceful dissent and that life, liberty, and the pursuit of happiness be extended to them as well. Whether intentional or not, omitting them from the narrative created a false understanding of America's shared and complex past.

The rise of the social history movement during the 1960s and 1970s led to exploration into ordinary people's lives. Historians scoured historical and archaeological records to glean new insights. They learned more about these groups, their intersections with each other, and their interactions with the ruling class. By the 1980s and 1990s, scholars began partnering with public historians deploying emerging technologies (like DNA and digital mapping) to create new exhibitions and programs to reach the public. On-going interdisciplinary research revealed unexpected familial connections and differences in diet, migration patterns, and health across race and status, among other things. Insights about how these marginalized people behaved during extraordinary times spurred a richer and far deeper understanding of our shared past. The remarkable stories uncovered of men and women from all walks of life, creeds, ethnicities, and hues were finally being woven

Old Bruton Church, Williamsburg, Virginia, in the Time of Lord Dunmore (detail), Alfred Wordsworth Thompson, 1893, oil on canvas. The Metropolitan Museum of Art, Gift of Mrs. A. Wordsworth Thompson, 1899

into the tapestry of the Revolutionary era and American history writ large.

I count myself fortunate to have witnessed the expansion of America's story—both as a young museum professional and an avid fan of museums. Working at Colonial Williamsburg in the 1980s and 1990s, it was my job to help millions of visitors understand what life was like for people of African descent who made up 52 percent of the colonial capital's population. Stating that fact alone left visitors dumbfounded and often intrigued to learn more. Most of them quickly connected the paradox of liberty and enslavement. They explored with us how marginalized people of every description claimed Patrick Henry's powerful decree as their own and embraced Thomas Jefferson's words as a national creed. Visitors began to see and understand that the promise of America was unkept for millions for more than a century and a half.

Now serving as the Executive Director of the Jamestown-Yorktown Foundation, I can attest that some challenges remain, but fortunately opportunities abound to share with audiences the amazing things we continue to learn. Covering the early English settlement through the Revolution's final battle at Yorktown, guests at our state's Revolutionary-era historic sites explore the roles of Indigenous Americans, Central West Africans, Europeans, and their descendants through this often-tumultuous period. The intersecting threads paint a far clearer picture of how and why ideas about the relationships between those who governed and the governed merged. For better or worse, the good, bad, and ugly parts of our history enable us to better evaluate how the nation evolved the way it did—and continues to do so. With the 250th anniversary of the Declaration of Independence upon us, museum and academic professionals along with community and civic leaders needed to decide how we could and should commemorate the event in Virginia.

In late 2018, museum professionals, Virginia Tribal members, Virginia Tourism Corporation, and Virginia Humanities convened to discuss opportunities for the coming 250th. Choosing the moniker "Revolutionary Virginia 250" (RevVA250), members understood that many key events leading up to the Declaration's ratification either occurred in Virginia or were led by Virginians. They also recognized that the document—principally authored by Jefferson—not only ushered in the American Revolution but also became a writ about the rights of humankind around the world. The Declaration of Independence had a profound impact on eighteenth-century global geopolitical and social dynamics, but it also became a global call regarding the relationship between the governed and governments well into the twenty-first century.

RevVA250 met numerous times to contemplate goals, collaborations, new scholarship, programs and exhibition ideas, and more. With unanimity, they stressed the importance of the commemoration being an opportunity for Virginians and visitors to gain a deeper understanding of this seminal event and its global ramifications. Members were adamant that only talking about Thomas Jefferson would be an opportunity missed.

They wanted people to understand that the United States' remarkable evolution was due to each generation of citizens of every hue and class using Jefferson's words to expand what it means to be an American. This was a lofty goal for certain, but one that everyone felt was obtainable.

As meetings continued, all understood the clear advantage Virginia has with its wealth of historical assets, world-class museums, and iconic and lesser-known historic sites. If handled properly, we could lead the national conversation. However, more practical considerations led to questions about how statewide activities should be organized and coordinated. We wanted to have a range of activities for all potential audiences, including teachers and their students, museum goers, history enthusiasts, and the public. RevVA250 also contemplated what the appropriate relationships between the Commonwealth of Virginia, non-profits, and localities should be. In the fall of 2019, leadership at the Jamestown-Yorktown Foundation worked with the Virginia Museum of History & Culture on behalf of the collaboration to seek legislation to create a statewide Virginia American Revolution 250 Commission.

When the Virginia General Assembly met in January 2020, there was considerable enthusiasm for a commission. Bipartisan support abounded and bills passed the State House and Senate easily. In mid-March 2020, representatives from RevVA250 met with the Secretary of Education and his staff and members of the legislative team to draft timelines and organizational milestones. Efforts stalled when the Covid-19 pandemic struck. Non-essential government operations shut down and historic sites around the state closed for at least fourteen weeks. Understanding the importance of the effort, work continued behind the scenes. When the legislation was enacted, the RevVA250 team began searching for a leader. The Jamestown-Yorktown Foundation initially served as the fiduciary and organizational steward through its Virginia Commemorations, Inc. (VCI) non-profit affiliate. VCI had managed successful statewide commemorations in the past. The next step was finding a leader to coordinate activities around the state and identify signature activities. The passed legislation also changed the name from RevVa250 to VA250 and initial funding was secured to support several initiatives.

Among the signature activities created for VA250 is the major exhibition, *Give Me Liberty: Virginia & The Forging of a Nation*. An extraordinary partnership between the Virginia Museum of History & Culture and the Jamestown-Yorktown Foundation, the exhibit provides depth, nuance, and an inclusive narrative based on stellar scholarship. In addition, the team created smaller panel versions to distribute to schools and libraries around the state. This accompanying book ensures that Virginia's commemoration of the Semiquincentennial and its legacies are available to those yearning for knowledge and insights into how we became Americans.

Christy S. Coleman
Executive Director
Jamestown-Yorktown Foundation

Acknowledgments

This publication, a companion to Jamestown-Yorktown Foundation and the Virginia Museum of History & Culture's joint exhibition, *Give Me Liberty: Virginia & The Forging of a Nation*, was made possible with generous support from *The Conrad M. Hall Endowment for the Study of Virginia History*.

The exhibition was additionally made possible with generous support from Virginia's American Revolution 250 Commission, its presenting sponsor. The Virginia Museum of History & Culture (VMHC) also wishes to recognize exhibition sponsors: Mr. & Mrs. E. Claiborne Robins, Jr., Melanie Trent De Schutter, Conrad Mercer Hall, Lisa & Bill Moore, the Helen Marie Taylor Charitable Foundation, Inc., The Cabell Foundation, The Mary Morton Parsons Foundation, Anne Mullen Orrell Charitable Trust, and The June H. Guthrie Foundation. Jamestown-Yorktown Foundation (JYF) wishes to recognize exhibition sponsors: York County, Virginia, and the Carter Cabell Chinnis Foundation.

This overall joint commemorative project benefitted greatly from feedback provided by an engaged group of stakeholders, including teachers, museum colleagues, and community organization leaders. JYF and VMHC wish to thank: Kara Canaday, CEO, Virginia Tribal Education Consortium; Dr. Sabrina Dent, Director, Baptist Joint Committee; Julie Laghi, Asian American Society of Central Virginia; Caroline Legros, Manager of Civics Education, VMHC's John Marshall Center for Constitutional History & Civics; Rebecca Martin, Director of Education, Gunston Hall; Carrie O'Hanlon, civics & economics teacher, Phenix PreK-8 School; Cameron Patterson, Senior Partner for Strategic Initiatives, Robert Russa Moton Museum; Kyle Stetz, Director of Education, James Madison's Montpelier; Gayle Jessup White, Community Engagement Officer, Thomas Jefferson Foundation; and Allison Wickens, Vice President, Education, George Washington's Mount Vernon.

An all-star cast of scholars provided invaluable assistance with exhibition content development in addition to authoring the essays for this publication. JYF and VMHC are deeply indebted to the following for their time and expertise: Dr. Antonio T. Bly, Peter H. Shattuck Endowed Chair in Colonial American History and Professor, California State University, Sacramento; Dr. Steven A. Harris-Scott, Academic Director, George Mason University; Dr. Woody Holton, Professor of History, University of South Carolina; Dr. Sarah E. McCartney, Assistant Teaching Professor, Harrison Ruffin Tyler Department of History and National Institute of American History & Democracy, College of William & Mary; Dr. Alan Taylor, Thomas Jefferson Foundation Chair (Emeritus), University of Virginia; Dr. Jonathan W. White, Professor of American Studies, Christopher Newport University; and Dr. Karin Wulf, Beatrice and Julio Mario Santo Domingo Director and Librarian, John Carter Brown Library, and Professor of History, Brown University.

This project was a collaborative effort shared by JYF and VMHC. Many talented staff from these institutions worked together to develop and execute the exhibition and publication. From JYF, we would like to express our thanks to: Felicia Abrams, School Programs Manager; Harvey Bakari, Curator of Black History and Culture; Lisa Bishop, Registrar; Kate Gruber, Manager, Curatorial Services; Travis Henline, Curator of Indigenous History and Culture; Heather Hower, Director, Digital Media Services; Dr. Mariruth Leftwich, Senior Director, Museum Operations and Education; and Jaie Pizzetti, Education Specialist, Learning and Community Engagement.

From the VMHC team, we wish to thank: Heather Beattie, Collections Manager; Ajana Bradshaw, Exhibitions Coordinator; Bryan Condra, Exhibit Designer; Maggie Creech, Director of Education; Graham Dozier, Manager of Publications & Scholarship; Danni Flakes, Photographer; Sam Florer, Manager of Public Programs; Dr. James Herrera-Brookes, Melanie Trent De Schutter Sr. Director of Research & Publications; Dale Kostelny, Exhibit Production Manager; Rebecca Rose, Director of Collections Management; Stacy Rusch, Senior Conservator; Adam Scher, Lisa & Bill Moore Vice President for Collections, Exhibitions & Research; Christina Smith, Collections Management Assistant; and Andy Talkov, Senior Director of Curatorial Affairs.

Finally, our profound appreciation goes out to all who support the Virginia Museum of History & Culture and the Jamestown-Yorktown Foundation and our efforts to tell the rich and full story of this Commonwealth. It is our sincere hope that this exhibition and publication will contribute to that worthy endeavor.

Jamie O. Bosket
President & CEO
Virginia Museum of History & Culture

Christy S. Coleman
Executive Director
Jamestown-Yorktown Foundation

Ruins of Jamestown (detail), John Gadsby Chapman, 1834, oil on wood. VMHC

Introduction

To commemorate the 250th anniversary of the Declaration of Independence and to highlight Virginia's leadership in the American Revolution, the Jamestown-Yorktown Foundation and the Virginia Museum of History & Culture partnered to create the signature exhibition, *Give Me Liberty: Virginia & The Forging of a Nation*. The exhibition explores the people, sites, and events that created a new nation and examines what concepts of liberty meant for different peoples in the 1770s and 1780s. It highlights the compelling stories of individuals and families, illustrating the difficult choices that confronted all people—Indigenous peoples, free and enslaved Virginians, and white people of every class. Importantly, it also demonstrates that the journey to fully realize American liberty is ongoing work.

This collection of essays, written by leading scholars of the period, serves as a valuable companion to the exhibition. Each essay complements themes that are reflected in the exhibition's stories, artifacts, and images that were carefully chosen to bring a new depth of understanding of Virginia's Revolutionary era. They provide a closer look at the complex origins of American unrest and investigate its consequences for people, families, and institutions.

The American Revolution was never a foregone conclusion. Instead, it was the culmination of rising colonial discontent that grew over decades. As the policies of Great Britain led American colonists to feel that they were unjustly treated, they began to protest and act. Woody Holton illustrates in his essay that it was the British Crown's punitive measures in suppression of American protests that caused a "reprisal spiral" and became the final push that steered colonists toward independence. In Virginia, colonists demonstrated their support for the people of Boston after such punitive measures were imposed upon them. This led to a rift with the colony's governor, Lord Dunmore, who disbanded the representative assembly.

While Virginians protested British policies in the east, in 1774 they launched attacks against Indigenous tribes on the colony's western border—Dunmore's War, a conflict with the Shawnee and other Indigenous nations to control western lands. Immediately following, Virginia militiamen and others on the borderlands issued a series of resolutions in support of American liberty. In her essay, Sarah E. McCartney details the revolutionary sentiments of "backcountry" Virginians living along the borderlands. She demonstrates that western Virginians were full participants in revolutionary political maneuverings and had equal interests in their outcomes, and that their interests were based around their lived experiences of settlement and frontier defense.

The coming of the war affected all people in both the American colonies and Indigenous nations. As rising tensions with the British government became open conflict, individuals and families faced difficult choices about loyalty, family, freedom, and liberty. As Karin Wulf explores in her essay, Virginians understood the American Revolution as a family matter. She illustrates that colonists, free and enslaved Afro-Virginians, and

Indigenous peoples felt the impact of the war most profoundly in a family context, with dislocation, family crisis, death, and loss. Families and tribes often became divided in their loyalties, and the Revolution became a civil war that tore them apart.

Enslaved Virginians were among those who faced tough decisions. After the British Crown declared the American colonies in rebellion, Virginia's Governor Dunmore issued a proclamation promising freedom to enslaved people of rebel owners who joined the British cause. As Antonio T. Bly points out, enslaved Virginians had agency and were actively engaged in the Revolution's politics. He demonstrates that they, in fact, enacted their own revolutions by taking a chance for freedom as they protested slavery with their feet. Bly examines the ways in which Afro-Virginians learned and communicated about the conflict and formed their own revolutionary ideologies before they decided to act on them.

The Revolutionary era was a time of profound change in North America. Although war was being fought on battlefields, other revolutions were occurring elsewhere, including the pulpit. Before the American Revolution, the Church of England served as the officially sanctioned church in Virginia. All property owners were taxed to pay for the church, and no one could vote or hold political office without church membership, which in effect made the Anglican Communion the official church in Virginia. Alan Taylor demonstrates that all that changed in 1776 when Virginia adopted a new Bill of Rights, which included the "free exercise of religion, according to the dictates of conscience." This was a profound shift that championed individual liberty and helped facilitate a new social order. Taylor notes that creating the strictest separation of church and state in the new nation was "white Virginians' proudest accomplishment."

In the long course of history, 250 years is a small portion of time. Yet so much can occur during this brief space. For Americans, the last 250 years have shaped and defined our young nation. From our revolutionary beginnings through two and a half centuries of struggles and victories, setbacks and accomplishments, each generation has fought to make manifest our founding ideals that "all men are created equal," rooted in our inalienable rights of "life, liberty, and the pursuit of happiness." Like the nation's founders, current and future generations must define their own notions of liberty and take the actions necessary to secure them. The struggle to achieve American liberties that began in the eighteenth century continues today. What does liberty mean to you?

Travis Henline
Curator of Indigenous History and Culture
Jamestown-Yorktown Foundation

Harvey Bakari
Curator of Black History and Culture
Jamestown-Yorktown Foundation

Chapter 1

When Britain Reformed its Empire, Virginians Resisted—and the War Came

Woody Holton

Between 1763 and 1776, impassioned denunciations of how Britain treated its American colonists gushed forth: not from the Americans, but from Parliament. Leaders of the more powerful chamber, the House of Commons, fought to transform the empire in four crucial areas, neatly summarized as the four Ts: taxes, territory, treasury notes (money), and trade. Parliament saw its changes as reforms, but to many white colonists, they looked like slavery—and these were people who knew slavery from wielding the lash. In response to Parliament's initiatives, a protest convention in Williamsburg, Virginia, in August 1774 harkened back to the status that colonists had enjoyed within the British empire up until 1763 and pled for the "Restoration and Continuance" of those good old days.[1]

In the eighteenth century, restoration was a loaded term, usually associated with the Restoration of England's Stuart monarchy in 1660, after a two-decade experiment in government without a king. But especially for Virginia gentlemen like Thomas Jefferson and George Washington—roughly the top 10 percent of the province's social and economic pyramid—preservation was the logical choice. After all, they had prospered under the old imperial regime.

If the impetus for change did not come from the gentry, where *did* it arise? Seemingly everywhere else. Parliament not only had its own ideas about transforming the imperial relationship but also channeled and amplified other, still more powerful, influences. The majority of Englishmen who could vote in parliamentary elections owed most of their wealth to land. But especially after England's union with Scotland in 1707, the United Kingdom became a commercial nation, and the loudest pipers calling

John Murray, fourth Earl of Dunmore (detail), Charles X. Harris, copied from the original portrait by Sir Joshua Reynolds, 1929, oil on canvas. VMHC, Bequest of Ambassador Alexander Wilbourne Weddell and Virginia Chase Steedman Weddell

The Bloody Massacre perpetrated in King Street Boston on March 5th, 1770, by a party of the 29th Regt, Paul Revere, 1770, engraving. Library of Congress

Parliament's tunes were Britain's merchant princes. The imperial government made it easier for metropolitan merchants to collect the money American farmers and traders owed them, removed all obstacles to the traffic in kidnapped Africans, and guaranteed metropolitan merchants a near monopoly of colonial trade.

Nor were commercial men the only ones Virginia gentlemen accused of exerting undue influence over Parliament. Ever since May 1607, when the *Discovery*, *Susan Constant*, and *Godspeed* anchored off Jamestown, an essential ingredient in the gentry's success had been westward expansion. Gentlemen sometimes described the territory they acquired as virgin land, but most of it was occupied and worked by Indigenous people. For decades, British officials supported American colonists' effort to extend the British empire into the American interior. But by the middle of the eighteenth century, military expenses consumed as much as 95 percent of the imperial budget. So, starting in 1758, London embarked on a new policy of trying to avoid costly wars against Indigenous nations by preventing British Americans from stealing their land. Parliament thus set its face against the income source that had produced, as George Washington observed in 1767, "the greatest Estates we have"—including much of his own.[2]

As angry as the colonists were at London's new provincial taxes and its unprecedented interference in their trade, territorial expansion, and emission of treasury notes, these four Ts did not convince Virginians to secede from the mother country. But freeholders were determined to return the imperial relationship to the status quo of 1762. They protested all of Parliament's innovations, sometimes violently. These demonstrations often thwarted British initiatives and always infuriated Parliament, which clamped down on the protestors, often with extreme violence. In Massachusetts, redcoats killed five colonial rioters on March 5, 1770, in the Boston Massacre and, five years later, about fifty militiamen in Lexington and Concord and all along the British march back to Boston. April 19, 1775, thus became not only the first battle of the Revolutionary War but also, for many colonists, the final argument for independence. Also in 1775, whites in the southernmost provinces (Georgia, South Carolina, North Carolina, and Virginia) harassed their governors, prompting all four to take refuge on British warships. In response, several governors and Royal Navy captains accepted enslaved southerners' offer of an informal alliance against the people who claimed to own them. It was not the American protestors' original grievances against Parliament that provoked them to sever ties with the United Kingdom. It was Britain's suppression of their protests. This escalating cycle of attacks from both sides may be summed up as a reprisal spiral.

What motivated Virginia, the most populous of Britain's twenty-six American colonies, to join twelve of the others in declaring independence? Not Parliament's fiscal, territorial, and commercial reforms, as loathsome as those were. Rather, the measures that Members of Parliament saw as reforms provoked

CANTONMENT of HIS MAJESTY'S FORCES in N. AMERICA

ACCORDING TO THE DISPOSITION NOW MADE & TO BE COMPLEATED AS SOON AS PRACTICABLE

taken from the General Distribution dated at New York 29th March 1766. By Dan. Paterson Ass.t Q.r M.r Gen.l
with the alterations to summer 1767 done in yellow.

LAKE SUPERIOR
Michillimakinac
L. HURON
L. MICHIGAN
LANDS RESERVED FOR THE INDIANS
Oswegatchie
L. ONTARIO
Niagara
Oswego
F.t Stanwix
NEW YORK
Albany
Detroit
60. 2 Bat.
L. ERIE
PENSYLVANIA
Elizabeth
Amboy
New York
F.t Pitt
42.
Philadelphia
16.
46. 22.
26.
MARYLAND
LOUISIANA
F.t Chartres
34.
OHIO R.
VIRGINIA
MISSISSIPPI R.
N. CAROLINA
F.t Prince George
No. 2.
F.t Charlotte
No. 3
S. CAROLINA
No. 4
F.t Augusta
CharlesTown
No. 6.
PART of NEW MEXICO
Tombecbe
GEORGIA
Natches
Apalachi
No. 7
W. FLORIDA
Ibbeville
Mobile
Pensacola
21.
31.
E. FLORIDA
F.t Frederica
No. 5
S.t Augustine
9.
GULF of MEXICO
ATLANTIC
Providence

72-2042

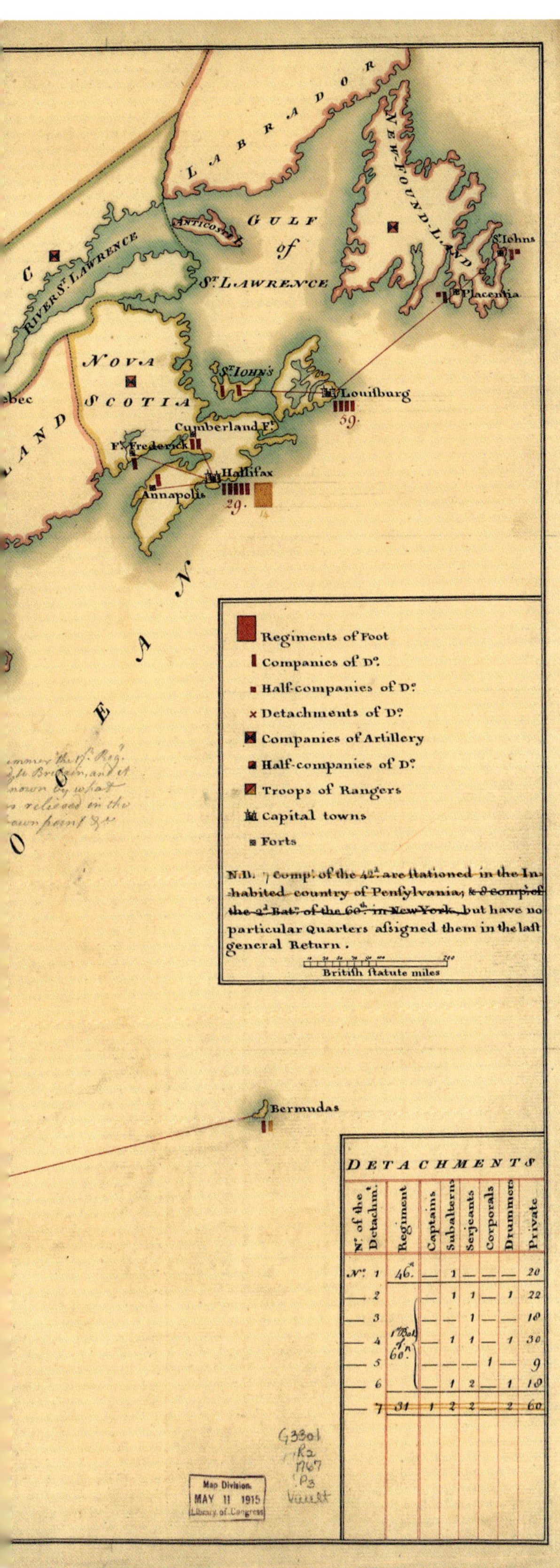

Cantonment of His Majesty's Forces in N. America according to the disposition now made & to be completed as soon as practicable taken from the General Distribution dated at New York 29th. March 1766, 1767. Library of Congress

alarming colonial protests that in turn stirred Parliament to hit the Americans with the punitive measures that convinced them they had no choice but to exit the empire.

Indians, Slaves, Merchants, and the Four Ts of Colonial Protest

Until the mid-eighteenth century, the British government encouraged and assisted its American colonists' westward expansion. This not only fed imperial pride but also seemed to foster Britain's commercial expansion. Most of all, every additional armed British subject who ventured out to the west strengthened the empire's competition against its dreaded colonial rivals, especially France.

But then British officers became convinced that winning the Seven Years' War (1754–63), known in America as the French and Indian War, required them to execute an about-face. The British could deprive France of some of its Indigenous allies simply by meeting some of the Indians' demands. At the Treaty of Easton in October 1758, representatives of the Upper Ohio Valley nations, especially the Shawnees and Delawares, made peace with the British in return for their promise to remain east of the Appalachian Mountains. The agreement did in fact persuade many Indigenous warriors to break off their alliance with the French. A few joined the British, but many more simply turned neutral, which was all London needed. Pleased with the success of its new policy, the British government decided to stand by its promise to Native American leaders. What royal officials did not anticipate was that this decision would give birth to two of the colonists' most urgent grievances against Parliament: its limits on their westward expansion and, less obviously, its effort to levy taxes on them.

At the end of most colonial wars, the soldiers Britain sent to America got to go home. But in December 1762, just three months before the peace treaty that ended the Seven Years' War, George III's cabinet made the extraordinary decision to keep 10,000 troops in America indefinitely. Some were there to prevent and put down rebellions, whether by enslaved workers in the Caribbean or conquered French subjects in Canada. But the largest number would guard the western frontier, not only protecting the colonists from Native warriors but also enforcing the government's promise not to encroach on the Native land west of the Appalachian Mountains. The *Annual Register*'s summary of the troops' mission was strange but succinct: "awing as well as protecting the Indian nations."[3]

In May 1763, a broad coalition of Native nations in what is now the Midwest rebelled against the British. Leadership of the revolt was widely dispersed, but whites came to know it as Pontiac's Rebellion. Recognizing that one of the rebels' most pressing grievances was continuing encroachment on their land, the Privy Council strengthened the Appalachian barrier to colonial settlement with a formal proclamation. Enforcing the Proclamation of 1763 thenceforth became a principal mission for the 10,000 troops that remained in North America after the Seven Years' War. But because those troops were also

THE

BRITISH STAMP

PROCURED FROM THE BRITISH GOVERNMENT

BY JOSEPH R. INGERSOLL

PRESENTED

TO THE

HISTORICAL SOCIETY OF VIRGINIA

BY THE

HISTORICAL SOCIETY OF PENNA: Jan: 1856.

British stamp procured from British Government by Joseph R. Ingersoll, 1765. VMHC, Gift of the Historical Society of Pennsylvania

there to prevent Native warriors from attacking colonial settlements east of the mountains—serving as a human wall—British officials and Members of Parliament decided to make the colonists pay for them. That meant taxing them.

The first two taxes that Parliament tried to impose on American colonists were the American Duties (often called Sugar) Act of 1764 and the Stamp Act of 1765. Most textbooks assert that both laws were aimed at shrinking the enormous debt that Britain had compiled during the Seven Years' War, but the text of the American Duties and Stamp Acts made it clear that their real purpose was to pay for British troops.[4]

As expensive as the 10,000 soldiers were, they were not numerous enough to stop colonial families from crossing the Proclamation Line and establishing farms. But they *were* effective against Virginians seeking to make or enhance their fortunes by speculating in Native American land. Just as you cannot sell your car if you cannot find the title, so the Proclamation of 1763 prevented speculators from taking title to the land they claimed and, without that, no one would pay them for it.

Native Americans defending their land thus indirectly but powerfully contributed to British colonists' grievances against their mother country. The Proclamation of 1763 infuriated Virginia land speculators like George Washington, Thomas Jefferson, Patrick Henry, and James Madison. And it was in hopes of avoiding war with Native rebels that Parliament stationed thousands of soldiers on the frontier, a decision that in turn led to the adoption of the Revenue and Stamp Acts, setting off the battle over taxation without representation. Indigenous Americans thus contributed to two of the four Ts summarizing colonists' grievances against Parliament: its efforts to tax Americans, even though they chose none of its members, and its crackdown on territorial expansion.

The British mercantile elite rounded out the colonists' list of grievances by persuading Parliament to crack down on them in the crucial areas of treasury notes and trade. By the 1760s, even many Virginians like Thomas Jefferson, who during his lifetime claimed ownership of 600 fellow humans, had joined a campaign to halt the trafficking of additional kidnapped Africans to North America. The enslavers' claims to oppose the Atlantic slave trade on humanitarian grounds are easily ridiculed, but many slaveholders liked to think of themselves as more humane than the rest. That meant not separating Black families—except, of course, when exceptional opportunities were offered. It also required them to oppose the indescribable Middle Passage across the Atlantic, where crew members sent below to spoon out slop complained that there was too little air down there to keep their lanterns lit.

Established enslavers like Jefferson also had economic incentives to shut off the flow of kidnapped Africans: it risked reducing the value of the human property they already possessed, and setting more people to work growing Virginia's staple, tobacco, threatened to lower its price. The African trade was also said to entail other economic evils, but the most passionate pleas against it focused on the danger that enslaved people might someday, as William Byrd II put it in 1736,

Petition, 1772, to King George III requesting a ban on the importation of slaves, 1772. VMHC

To the King's most Excellent Majesty.

The humble Address of the House of Burgesses of Virginia.

Most Gracious Sovereign.

We your Majesty's dutiful and loyal Subjects the Burgesses of Virginia, now met in General Assembly, beg Leave with all Humility, to approach your Royal Presence.

The many Instances of your Majesty's benevolent Intentions and most gracious Disposition to promote the Prosperity and Happiness of your Subjects in the Colonies encourage us to look up to the Throne, and implore your Majesty's paternal Assistance in averting a Calamity of a most alarming Nature.

The Importation of Slaves into the Colonies from the Coast of Africa hath long been considered as a Trade of great Inhumanity, and, under its present Encouragement, we have too much reason to fear will endanger the very Existence of your Majesty's American Dominions.

We are sensible that some of your Majesty's Subjects in Great-Britain may reap Emoluments from this Sort of Traffick, but when we consider that it greatly retards the Settlement of the Colonies with more useful Inhabitants, and may, in Time, have the most destructive Influence, we presume to hope that the Interest of a few will be disregarded, when placed in Competition with the Security and Happiness of such Numbers of your Majesty's dutiful and loyal Subjects.

Deeply impressed with these Sentiments, we most humbly beseech your Majesty to remove all those Restraints on your Majesty's Governors of this Colony which inhibit their assenting to such Laws, as might check so very pernicious a Commerce. Your Majesty's ancient Colony and Dominion of Virginia hath at all Times and upon every Occasion been entirely devoted to your Majesty's sacred Person and Government, and we cannot forego this Opportunity of renewing those Assurances of the truest Loyalty and warmest Affection, which we have so often, with the greatest Sincerity, given to the best of Kings, whose Wisdom and Goodness we esteem the surest Pledges of the Happiness of all his People.

Peyton Randolph Speaker

"tinge our rivers as wide as they are with blood." By 1776, 40 percent of Virginians were enslaved, and many whites perceived slaves born in Africa—those who had tasted freedom—as especially dangerous.[5]

For all these reasons, the House of Burgesses repeatedly tried to increase its tax on every African entering the colony, but most of these efforts were overturned by royal officials. So, in 1772, the burgesses unanimously petitioned the home government to abolish the Atlantic slave trade altogether. The petition got nowhere with Members of Parliament or their leaders, whose far higher priority was securing the income of the British slave traders—a "few African corsairs" (pirates), as Jefferson called them.

Human trafficking was not the only transatlantic trade that Parliament protected. Its statutes forced Americans to sell their tobacco only to British merchants—even though 80 percent was then reshipped to the European continent—and to buy manufactured goods from them as well. The so-called Navigation Acts were one of the grievances behind Bacon's Rebellion in 1676, but after that, Virginians only grumbled about them—that is, until 1764, when Parliament started trying to tax them as well. Writing on behalf of the House of Burgesses in 1775, Jefferson made Britain a surprising offer. Although free Virginians could never consent to being taxed by Parliament, because they were not represented there, the burgesses *were* willing to help pay for colonial administration and defense (including the troops at the Anglo-Indian border) by annually voting subsidies to Parliament. But there was a catch: in return for these subsidies, the mother country would have to grant Virginians "a free trade with all the world." In fact, the colonists would be thrilled to make that deal, Jefferson wrote, because Britain's "monopoly of our trade . . . brings greater loss to us and benefit to them than the amount of our proportional contributions to the common defence."[6]

The colonists did not oppose British taxation because they were stingy, but because they could not acquiesce in the precedent that they could be taxed by a body, Parliament, in which they were not represented and never could be. But free Americans also saw parliamentary taxation as the straw that broke the camel's back. Especially in the principal tobacco colonies, Virginia and Maryland, the greater burden that the camel already carried was the British merchants' monopoly of their trade. It is impossible to understand Virginia's road to revolution without taking account of the English and Scottish merchant princes' power over Parliament.

The Navigation Acts were only one instance in which Virginians' political dependence on the mother country made them economically dependent. Another was the colony's money supply. Like most other provinces, Virginia periodically printed paper money, primarily to pay for colonial wars. But paper currency often depreciated, sometimes even leading to the kind of runaway inflation we associate with failed states like Weimar Germany. Inflation meant that all along the credit chain, from the crossroads storekeeper in Virginia to the giant mercantile firms in British cities like Liverpool, London, and Glasgow, merchants who sold goods on credit got paid back in money that was worth much less than what they had lent out. That is why, in 1764, merchants in the mother country persuaded Parliament to adopt the Currency Act, which prohibited the colonies from printing paper notes—technically "treasury notes." The Currency Act was thus the last of our four Ts, because it infuriated the colonists by subjecting them to crippling *de*flation.[7]

British merchants also contributed to the free Virginians' animus against the British government in ways that were less direct and less deliberate. Tens of thousands of free Virginians spent their entire adult lives in debt to British merchants. Many Loyalists, and some Progressive historians around the turn of the twentieth century, posited a simple explanation for the Chesapeake colonists' enthusiasm for rejecting the British empire: they did it to skate out on their debts. But this cynical claim has been refuted by historians pointing out that the Revolution did not officially quash the debts; it only delayed payment (with, to be sure, many being written off in the meantime). Indeed, at least two of the mechanisms by which free Virginians protested British taxes and other innovations helped them *pay off* their debts. These were nonimportation and nonexportation.[8]

On June 29, 1767, Parliament adopted the Townshend duties—taxes on tea, glass, lead, paper, and painters' colors. In response, many colonists boycotted British merchandise: not just the newly taxed items but also cloth, which was their leading import from the mother country. The obvious and most oft-stated reason to stop buying British wares was to apply economic pressure on British merchants to lean on Parliament to repeal the Townshend duties. But many supporters of the boycott candidly acknowledged that it would also serve another purpose. Signers of one non-consumption agreement noted that it would additionally enable them to escape their "embarrassed & distressed Circumstances"; their slogan was "Save your MONEY, and you save your COUNTRY!"[9]

George Washington also expected the buyers' boycott to help colonists in two distinct ways. Ten years before Auguste Comte coined the term *sociology*, Washington shared with his neighbor George Mason some keen sociological—and possibly autobiographical—insights. In theory, a man trapped in debt could just curtail his expenses, but it was not that easy. "[F]or how can I, *says he*, who have lived in such & such a manner change my method? I am ashamed to do it." So, to keep up appearances, the indebted spendthrift keeps on spending beyond his means until his exasperated creditors force him to sell everything he owns. But an anti-British boycott would both pressure Parliament to repeal the Townshend Acts and at the same time give debtors "a pretext to live within bounds." "[E]xtravagant & expensive" Virginians could forgo luxury while still preserving their honor.[10]

Even as many Virginians vowed to buy less British merchandise, others sought to reduce their debts by holding their tobacco back from the market. Stored tobacco eventually spoils, but it can last a year or more, and that gave growers a leg-up in their perennial battle against buyers over the price of the weed. *One* tobacco farmer could not affect the price, even if he withheld his entire crop. But if all or most of the tobacco growers in a neighborhood refused to sell, then one or two of the British captains who had come for their crops might, in their eagerness to turn their ships around, offer a penny or two more per pound. Newspaper writers occasionally broached the idea, but the first growers known to have tried it lived around Bladensburg, Maryland. The idea soon crossed the Potomac River into Virginia, where local crop-withholding associations may have achieved modest success.

Near the end of 1772, Virginians received a powerful new incentive to hold their tobacco back. A recession swept through the entire British Atlantic, reducing the price of tobacco by nearly 40 percent. At this stage, what tobacco growers lacked was not motivation but organization. No boycott could succeed while ship captains could simply weigh anchor and try the next river. Growers needed a crop-withholding association that spanned the entire Chesapeake. But creating one seemed impossible.[11]

Then in the spring of 1774, to punish Bostonians for the Boston Tea Party, Parliament adopted the battery of legislation that Americans called the Intolerable Acts. Now numerous colonists started talking about halting exports to Britain right along with imports. In October 1774, delegates from every colony but Georgia gathered at Carpenters' Hall in Philadelphia and adopted a near-total ban on trade with the mother country. But the nonexportation clause contained two important exceptions. One was for rice, which was selling well;

Americans throwing the Cargoes of the Tea Ships into the River, at Boston, from W. D. Cooper, *History of North Americas*, 1789, engraving. Library of Congress

South Carolina delegates had guaranteed the continued shipment by threatening to boycott the boycott, at one point even walking out of Carpenters' Hall.[12]

The other exception to nonexportation postponed the tobacco boycott to September 10, 1775, allowing farmers to market their 1774 crops. As everyone knew they would, European merchants anticipating the cessation of exports stocked up on tobacco, richly rewarding the growers' bold effort to "revise the value of their staple." The high price of the weed drew forth whole warehouses' worth of tobacco that farmers had been holding back for years, boosting the 1775 tobacco shipment above one hundred million pounds: colonial Chesapeake's second largest ever. Yet, merchants were so determined to lay up tobacco for the lean years ahead that the price continued to rise, in seeming defiance of basic economic law. Even in combination with nonimportation, nonexportation did not force Parliament to repeal the Coercive Act. But tobacco withholding did fulfill the expectations of one of its earlier advocates, William Lee, who had promised that it would yield not just political but "pecuniary" benefits.[13]

Selling all that high-priced tobacco while importing only £2,000 (sterling) worth of British merchandise in 1775, Marylanders as well as Virginians dramatically shrank their debts. Richard Champion, a Bristol, England, merchant, was not exaggerating much when he claimed that in the single year 1775, Americans reduced their debt to British merchants from £6 million to £2 million.[14]

The House of Commons, 1793–94, Anton Hickel, 1793–95, oil on canvas. National Portrait Gallery, London, Given by Francis Joseph I, Emperor of Austria, 1885

Parliamentary Punishment and American Independence

Free Virginians hated the Proclamation Line, the Currency Act, the Stamp Act, and the other policies that Parliament and its leaders tried to impose on them in the 1760s. But taken together, these measures were not enough to convince colonists that they ought to declare independence. So how did free Virginians go from laboring to *restore* the imperial regime of 1762, as they did right up through the summer of 1774, to declaring independence two summers later? The answer lies in the Declaration of Independence, specifically in Congress's twenty-six grievances. Most of these did *not* address the colonial taxes and other reforms—the four Ts—that Parliament had adopted in the 1760s. Rather, that which provoked free American colonists to declare independence from the British government was the punishments it inflicted on Americans for resisting those earlier initiatives.

Everyone knows how the reprisal spiral worked in Massachusetts. Parliament's taxes and its crackdown on molasses smuggling motivated colonists to do things like tar and feather tax collectors and throw 342 chests of British tea into their harbor. Those protests in turn provoked British crackdowns like the Boston Massacre and the redcoats' fateful march to Concord on the night of April 18–19, 1775. But it had not been the smuggling crackdown or the stamp or tea taxes that led Massachusetts residents to become Whigs (the Americans who resisted British rule often called themselves *Whigs*, after the parliamentary faction that sought to check monarchical power, and many historians prefer that term, because *rebels* is biased against them and *patriots* is loaded in their favor). It was the home government's violent response to Whig protests.

Virginians shared northerners' concerns but also lodged more pressing complaints of their own. Ironically, the grievance that most angered white Virginians first entered the written record in Boston. On September 22, 1774, Abigail Adams wrote her husband John, who was off at Congress, reporting that Black Bostonians had "got an Irishman to draw up a petition to the Govener telling him they would fight for him provided he would arm them and engage to liberate them if he conquerd." Two months later, James Madison offered a similar report: that enslaved people near Montpelier, his home in the Virginia Piedmont, recently "met together & chose a leader who was to conduct them when the English Troops should arrive."[15]

On the night of April 20–21, 1775, Black Virginians played a central if often overlooked role in one of Virginia's most significant stepping-stones to independence: the removal of eighteen half-barrels of gunpowder from the cone-roofed brick powder magazine in the center of Williamsburg. Lord Dunmore, not yet aware that he was to be Virginia's last royal governor, had crewmen from a British warship seize this ammunition at the end of the week when whites in the James River watershed (which includes Richmond, Petersburg, Williamsburg, and Norfolk) reported more slave conspiracies than in any previous week in Virginia history. Many white colonists suspected that their governor's timing was no coincidence, that he had taken the powder just in time to make them vulnerable to the enslaved rebels. And the governor seemed to confirm that suspicion when he threatened to free the enslaved people if he or other royal officials were harmed. One man testified that Dunmore had forfeited "the Confidence of the People not so much for having taken the Powder as for the declaration he made of raising and freeing the Slaves."[16]

Dunmore's threat was idle. When two enslaved Virginians knocked on the door of the Governor's Palace in Williamsburg and offered to fight on Dunmore's side, he turned them away, saying he would whip them if they came back. But enslaved people kept coming. Among them was Joseph Harris, a river pilot from Hampton. One night late in July 1775, Harris escaped to a Royal Navy squadron and went to work piloting a warship called the *Liberty*. On September 2, 1775, a hurricane swept through Chesapeake Bay, driving the *Liberty* ashore near Hampton, a hotbed of resistance to British rule. The shipwrecked crew included not only Harris but also Matthew Squire, the commander of the *Liberty*'s mother ship. For Squire, captivity would be humiliating. For Harris, it might mean death, because in white Virginians' eyes he was not just a runaway but a rebel.[17]

Harris procured a canoe from a Hampton slave and rowed Squire across Hampton Roads, back to Norfolk and the safety of the British fleet. On October 27, Squire's squadron attacked Hampton.

John Murray, fourth Earl of Dunmore, Charles X. Harris, copied from the original portrait by Sir Joshua Reynolds, 1929, oil on canvas. VMHC, Bequest of Ambassador Alexander Wilbourne Weddell and Virginia Chase Steedman Weddell

bringing him to me in the aforeſaid County.

JOHN MAY.

RUN away from *Hampton*, on *Sunday* laſt, a luſty Mulatto Fellow named ARGYLE, well known about the Country, has a Scar on one of his Wriſts, and has loſt one or more of his fore Teeth; he is a very handy Fellow by Water, or about the Houſe, &c. loves Drink, and is very bold in his Cups, but daſtardly when ſober. Whether he will go for a Man of War's Man, or not, I cannot ſay; but I will give 40s. to have him brought to me. He can read and write.

NOVEMBER 2, 1775. JACOB WRAY.

RUN away from the Subſcriber, in *New Kent*, in the Year 1772, a ſmall new New Negro Man named GEORGE, about 40 Years of Age, mith a Nick in one Ear, and ſome Marks with the Whip. He was about *Williamſburg* till laſt Winter, but either went or was ſent to Lord *Dunmore*'s Quarter in *Frederick* County, and there paſſes for his Property. Whoever conveys him to me ſhall have 5l. Reward.

1|| JAMES MOSS.

STRAYED, or STOLEN, from the

Runaway enslaved advertisements, Virginia Gazette, November 4, 1775. VMHC

In the ensuing firefight, the Whigs captured Harris's vessel, along with "five white men, a woman, and two slaves." But Harris and the lieutenant commanding the boat escaped by plunging at the last instant into the Hampton River and swimming together to safety. That meant twice in two months that Harris had piloted his captain out of the Whigs' clutches.

So many Black Virginians joined Dunmore, who was desperately short on soldiers, that he formed them into what he called the Ethiopian Regiment. On November 15, the Whig militia from Princess Anne County (now Virginia Beach) attacked Dunmore's Black troops near Norfolk—and the Ethiopian Regiment won. Col. Joseph Hutchings, the commander of the Princess Anne militia, was captured by one of his own former slaves. Only after his unofficial Black allies had proved themselves in all these ways did the governor make their alliance official. Later that same day, November 15, he issued an emancipation proclamation offering freedom to rebels' slaves who would fight for their king. Dunmore directed it at slaves and servants "able and willing to bear Arms," but about half of the enslaved who escaped to him were women and children.[18]

As many as a thousand self-emancipated Black Virginians joined Dunmore over the next eight months, but at no time did he have more than half that number, because the Whigs compelled the governor's force to spend most of its time on crowded ships or beachheads, and they soon fell victim to infectious disease. After scores died of smallpox, Dunmore inoculated the rest. But a fever—possibly yellow or typhoid fever, but most likely some combination of malaria and typhus—continued the mass killing. Early in August, Dunmore concluded that this epidemic had left him no choice but to sail the remnants of the Ethiopian Regiment,

Death of Major Peirson, January 6, 1781, John Singleton Copley, 1783, oil on canvas. © Tate, London 2024

along with the few whites who had rallied to his standard, north to British headquarters on Staten Island, where they were immediately accused of spreading yellow fever.[19]

On September 15, 1776, the British captured New York City, which they held for the rest of the war. The Black Virginians who had escaped to Governor Dunmore would be joined there by other self-emancipated slaves, making New York City the largest Black community north of the Rio Grande. When the United States regained New York in the Paris peace talks of 1782–83, British vessels carried off about 3,000 Black Americans—some to London and other ports in the mother country but most to colonies that had remained loyal, especially Nova Scotia. Mistreated there by their fellow Loyalists but unwilling to be carried back to the United States, 1,200 of the Black Loyalists accepted a British invitation to found a new colony, Sierra Leone, on the west coast of Africa. We know of exactly one African-born former slave who made it back to his hometown, reappearing as if from the dead. Far more typical of the Sierra Leonians was Harry Washington, the former property of George Washington, who led fellow colonists in a tax revolt.[20]

Back in Virginia during the winter of 1775–76, free Virginians pretended that Governor Dunmore, rather than enslaved Virginians, had initiated their partnership. Whigs fulminated at their governor for, in the words of Archibald Cary of Chesterfield County, "pointing a dagger to their Throats, through the hands of their Slaves." Though Dunmore was the only royal official who issued a formal emancipation proclamation at this stage, other southern governors joined Royal Navy captains in informally welcoming self-emancipated Black people to their ranks. Dunmore and other British officials also cooperated with Native American leaders seeking to keep white settlers off their land.[21]

These "alliances," as Edmund Burke would later call them, infuriated even Americans who opposed slavery—people like Abigail Adams and Thomas Paine. In *Common Sense*, which appeared in January 1776, Paine predicted that "tens of thousands" of white Americans "would think it glorious to expel . . . that barbarous and hellish power, which hath stirred up the Indians and Negroes to destroy us." Just as Paine predicted, numerous whites' anger at Governor Dunmore turned them against the government he represented. William Byrd III's first response to the imperial conflict was to seek a commission in the British Army. But after Dunmore offered freedom to rebels' slaves, Cary noted, Byrd "made an offer of his services" to the Whigs. The Anglo-Black alliance had the same effect on whites in other colonies. "The dread of instigated insurrections," the Whig committee in New Hanover County, North Carolina, declared on June 19, 1775, "are causes sufficient to drive an oppressed people to the use of arms."[22]

For twelve years, white Virginians had resisted parliamentary innovations without aspiring to anything grander than the status quo of 1762. But when their royal governor punished this often-effective resistance by offering freedom to their enslaved, it pushed many white colonists further along

Thomas Paine, George Romney, engraving by William Sharp, 1793. Library of Congress

THOMAS PAINE.

the road to independence. There were other provocations as well. In the spring of 1776, Americans learned that the massive British army sailing toward them would include Hessian (German) mercenaries, who were considered even more vicious than redcoats. As Andrew Lawler has shown, it was the Whigs, not the British, who burned Virginia's largest port, Norfolk, but a Royal Navy squadron really did burn two towns in Massachusetts, and white Americans viewed all three conflagrations as British war crimes.[23]

For many elite Virginians, the final push toward independence came from an unexpected source: the lower-class white Virginians who up until this time had been content to follow the gentry's lead. But then ordinary farmers faced unprecedented privations and opportunities as the war came on, and they often found themselves openly defying the gentry. Imports ceased on December 1, 1774, and within a year, Virginians began to run out of the salt they needed to preserve their meat. Convinced that Piedmont merchants were holding back the little salt left to drive up the price (just as farmers had done with their tobacco), westerners assembled and marched east to seize it.

A summer 1775 Whig convention established minutemen battalions with gentry officers, but most Virginians found service in them intolerable. The numerous days of mandatory service made it impossible for enlisted men to maintain their farms, yet they were only paid while training or fighting. That was not enough to live on, so many refused to sign up. Landlords continued to charge rent even after nonexportation cut off tenants' income, leading to rent riots.

During the summer of 1775, the House of Burgesses met for the last time and Governor Dunmore abandoned his post, leaving Virginia without a provincial government. Power at the county level normally resided in the county courts. They continued to try criminal but not civil cases. At both the county and the provincial levels, Whig committees filled in the best they could, but committees are not governments.

The prospect of anarchy spread anxiety throughout the gentry class, but for some gentlemen, these fears spelled opportunity. In the spring of 1776, Virginians who wanted to formally secede from their mother country began to argue that doing so was the only way to restore order, for the simple reason that independence would allow for the establishment of a new government. When Landon Carter of Richmond County warned Francis Lightfoot Lee, who represented Virginia in Congress, that "licentiousness begins to prevail in Virga.," Lee did not try to reassure him. "The old Government being dissolved, & no new one substituted in its stead; Anarchy must be the consequence," he wrote. But making independence official would not only help the colonists defeat Britain but also foster "internal peace & good order."[24]

Small-scale landowners also pushed the gentry toward independence in a more direct way. In the April 1776 convention elections, they voted out several opponents of secession, replacing them with "determined men." When even Patrick Henry hesitated at the brink of independence, General Charles

Lee (no relation to the Virginia Lees) warned him that "the spirit of the people (except a very few in these lower parts of Virginia whose little blood has been suck'd out by musketoes) cry out for this Declaration." In the army, officers as well as enlisted men were "outrageous on the subject," Lee wrote, and disappointing them would be "dangerous." Landon Carter was convinced that the reason his less fortunate neighbors were so enthusiastic about separating from the mother country was that the colonies would not be alone in gaining independence. "[B]eing independt of the rich men," Carter imagined poor and middling freeholders saying, "eve[r]y man would then be able to do as he pleasd."[25]

On May 15, 1776, the Virginia convention instructed its representatives in Congress to formally propose independence. Meanwhile the convention delegates effectively declared independence on their own by drawing up a state constitution, prefaced by a Declaration of Rights. George Mason drafted the Declaration, but some of his fellow delegates identified a problem in the very first sentence, which affirmed that "all Men are born equally free and independent," possessing "certain inherent natural Rights." Many enslaved Virginians, they warned, would think this clause mandated their immediate emancipation. So, before approving the Declaration on June 12, the convention clarified that people's rights only kicked in "when they enter into a state of society." The qualification ran counter to natural rights philosophy, which holds that the freest men of all are those who have not formed societies, so when other provinces took Virginia's declaration of rights as models for their own, they fell back on Mason's original version.[26]

In the Declaration of Independence, Jefferson aimed his list of grievances squarely at George III, but he also made it clear that the king had not single-handedly driven the colonists to secede. Congress omitted Jefferson's few uses of the word *Parliament*, but no one doubted whom the delegates meant when they said King George had "combined with others to subject us to a jurisdiction foreign to our constitution, and unacknowledged by our laws." For the most part, the Declaration refers just as obliquely to British merchants, Native Americans, and African Americans. But they are there, both in the grievances describing the reforms Parliament had tried to adopt in the 1760s and in those that took aim at the punishment Parliament meted out to Americans for protesting those earlier reforms.

None of Britain's innovations in taxation, territory, treasury notes, and trade was intended solely to benefit the imperial government. Behind each was also what are known today as special interest groups. Jefferson and Congress complained that the British government had "endeavoured to prevent the population of these States" in several ways. It tried to thwart the colonists' westward expansion, admittedly for numerous reasons but especially to avoid another war against Native Americans. The principal beneficiaries of parliamentary legislation "cutting off our Trade with all parts of the world" were British merchants.[27]

In his longest and most passionate complaint in the Declaration—the only one in which he fell back on that ultimate expedient of the rookie writer: ALL CAPS—Jefferson claimed that George III had "waged cruel war against human nature itself, violating it's most sacred rights of life & liberty in the persons of a distant people who never offended him, captivating & carrying them into slavery in another hemisphere, or to incur miserable death in their transportation thither." Numerous critics have ridiculed this enslaver of 600 humans for insisting that the king had made him do it. But there was a grain of truth in Jefferson's indictment, because by this time, he and other large-scale enslavers had come out against the Atlantic (though not the domestic) slave trade. In his previous denunciations of the trafficking of kidnapped Africans, Jefferson had attributed its continuation to the powerful British merchants who drew their riches from it, but in the Declaration he placed all the blame on the king.

Jefferson also criticized Parliament and its American agents for everything they had done to punish white Americans for protesting their earlier innovations. In the same paragraph where he denounced the forced migration of Africans to North America, he castigated George III for "exciting those very people to rise in arms among us, and to purchase that liberty of which he has deprived them, & murdering the people upon whom he also obtruded them." Congress blotted out Jefferson's denunciation of the African trade and reduced his complaint about the Anglo-Black alliance to an incomprehensible euphemism that hid the considerable initiative that African Americans had exhibited over the previous two years: "He has excited domestic insurrections amongst us."

Having trimmed Jefferson's discussion of African Americans down to seven words, Congress merged it with his allegation that George III had manipulated another non-white group, "endeavour[ing] to bring on the inhabitants of our frontiers, the merciless Indian Savages." That phrase will stand forever as the ugliest line in America's most beautiful document.[28]

The first phrase from the Declaration of Independence to catch on throughout the country was not written by Jefferson. In its May 15 resolution, the Virginia convention had asked Congress "to declare the United Colonies free and independent states." Jefferson and Congress quoted Virginia's resolution in the final paragraph of the Declaration, and for the rest of the eighteenth century and well into the nineteenth, "Free and Independent States" was the Declaration of Independence's most quoted phrase. Hardly anyone cited "all men are created equal."[29]

But Jefferson's second paragraph did inspire one group of Americans: those who were campaigning against slavery. In fact, the first person to quote this section of the Declaration was the mixed-race Patriot soldier Lemuel Haynes, who used it as the epigraph for an antislavery pamphlet he called "Liberty Further Extended." The almanack maker Benjamin Banneker, also of mixed race, quoted "created equal" in an open letter calling on Jefferson to join the campaign against slavery. So too did numerous white abolitionists, especially Quakers.[30]

Simply by quoting "All men are created equal" so often, antislavery writers shifted the emphasis of the Declaration of Independence as dramatically as a spotlight swings from one actor to another. Suppose the focus of the Declaration had remained on independence from Britain. As the United States dissolved all doubts about its ability to stand on its own two feet, the Declaration's significance would have correspondingly diminished. By shifting the focus of our founding document from secession to equality, antislavery Americans made its significance both perpetual and global. They also turned a trophy into a challenge.

The elevation of the Declaration exalted Jefferson as well. The third president has often been called America's "Apostle of Freedom." That is a worthy tribute to the Virginian who wrote that "all men are created equal," but it is worth remembering that Jefferson owes this honor in large part to the Black and white antislavery writers who turned his ordinance of secession into a universal declaration of human rights.[31]

Lemuel Haynes, frontispiece illustration from *Sketches of the Life and Character of the Reverend Lemuel Haynes* by Timothy Mather Cooley, 1837. Library of Congress

Chapter 2

Revolutionary-era Sentiments in the Virginia Backcountry

Sarah E. McCartney

In Virginia's Revolutionary-era history, the region of Augusta County and Botetourt County is often overlooked. The area that encompassed the southern Shenandoah Valley, the Roanoke River Valley, and the New River Valley, and spanned from the Blue Ridge Mountains to the Ohio River, is lost between the political and military events in Williamsburg and Yorktown and conflicts on the western expanse of the Ohio Country. Similarly, the region is also overlooked as Revolutionary-era rhetoric and fiery language are often seen as originating from political debates in urban areas with an educated populace and gatherings of political elites in places like Independence Hall in Philadelphia, the Williamsburg Capitol, or even St. John's Church in Richmond. The subtext is that Virginians outside those arenas shouted "huzzah" in agreement but did not contribute to the discussion in a meaningful way. Despite these perceptions of physical and intellectual distance from the hubs of action, Virginians in the "near backcountry" saw themselves as fully part of Virginia's political maneuverings and they ensured that their sentiments of support were known as colonists moved from protest and words to action.[1]

In 1774, while counties throughout Virginia published resolutions focusing on the royal governor, Lord Dunmore, his dissolution of the House of Burgesses, and the meeting of the First Virginia Convention, residents from Augusta County and Botetourt County were focused on an expedition against the Shawnee with Lord Dunmore's support. When the backcountry settlers returned from what is known today as Dunmore's War with a victory and a treaty that Dunmore negotiated, they quickly turned their attention to colonial politics in the east. In resolutions published in the *Virginia Gazette* in March 1775, Augusta and Botetourt freeholders used passionate language that intertwined their sentiments about liberty with the lived experiences of a generation of backcountry settlement, revealing much

Shenandoah Valley (detail), William Louis Sonntag, late 1850s, oil on canvas. VMHC, Purchased with funds provided by Lora M. Robins

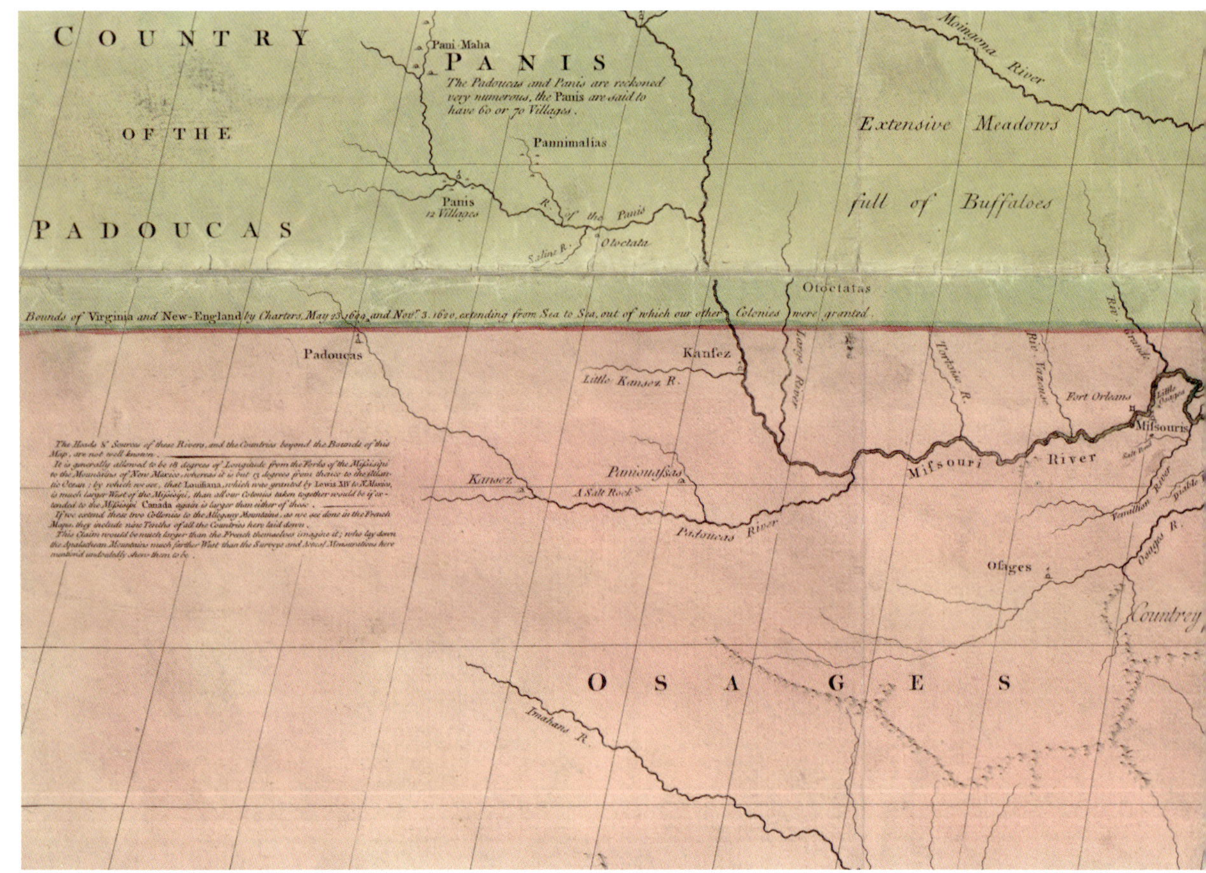

Detail showing the area of Augusta and Botetourt counties from *A map of the British and French dominions in North America, with the roads, distances, limits, and extent of the settlements, humbly inscribed to the Right Honourable the Earl of Halifax, 1755 . . .*, John Mitchell, 1755. Library of Congress

Quicapous
Miamis or Miammees
Iroquois R.
River Theakiki
Fort of the Miamis
The Rock or Rocher
The Antient Eriez were extirpated by the Iroquois upwards of 100 years ago, ever since which time they have been in Possession of L. Erie.
Halfway Cross
Sandoski
Canahogue
The Places called Licks and Lick Creeks are Salt water, which afford plenty of Salt to Man & Beast in these Inland Parts. The Resort of all sorts of Game, Huntsmen, Traders & Warriors, especially the Salt Ponds.
OHIO
Pimitiou L.
Pimiteoui
Copper Mine
R. Emicouen
Western Bounds
1170 m. from the Mouth of the Missisipi by Water
R. Cahoki
Cahokies
Tamaroas
F.t and Mission
Metchigamis
F.t Chartres
Kaskaskies
Mines of La Mote
C. St. Anthony
Great I.
Pickawillanees or Picts
Delaware T.
Hockhocken or Margarets T.
Delawares
Maguck
Lower Shawnoes
Pyankashees
Twightwees
Waughtanees
Great Wiaut
Little Wiaut
Wabache R.
VIRGINIA
The first Settlement of the English on the R. Ohio was at and about Alleghany 30 Years ago. Since which they have extended their Settlements from Shenango to Pickawillany.
Bever Ponds
to the falls with a very gentle Current
River Ohio about 1m. broad & 5 or 6 fathom deep
Forks of the Missisipi
Cuttawa
Catawba R.
Fredericks R.
Naked Cr.
Cumberland R.
Walkers
A Fine Level and Fertile Country of great Extent, by Accounts of the Indians and our People
920 m. Computed from the Sea
Augusta

about how they perceived themselves within both Virginia and the American colonies more broadly. By looking to the future and the past simultaneously, these resolutions demonstrate that the American Revolution was not just about a point in time in the 1770s, but an American journey. The resolutions illuminate the ways that journey reshaped backcountry Virginians' identities as Americans as they sought to preserve their home "happy, virtuous, and free."[2]

The Resolutions

In the winter of 1775, freeholders from Augusta and Botetourt counties documented their support for the growing patriotic fervor throughout the American colonies. The county freeholders, men who met the requirements for age, race, and landholding, had been busy with more local concerns related to Dunmore's War when most of Virginia's counties issued resolutions during the second half of 1774. As a second convention to be held in Richmond approached, Augusta and Botetourt counties published resolutions in three editions of the *Virginia Gazette* that noted their selection of delegates to the convention and provided them with instructions. As backcountry counties on the westernmost edge of Virginia's settlements, Augusta and Botetourt spanned vast stretches from the Blue Ridge Mountains of Virginia to the Ohio River, across present-day West Virginia. Although the county seats were in the Valleys of Virginia in the eastern parts of the counties, the east-to-west distance of these counties encompassed nearly half of Virginia.[3]

Botetourt County's Resolutions were published in Dixon and Hunter's *Virginia Gazette* on March 11, 1775, and Augusta County's Resolutions appeared in Pinkney's *Virginia Gazette* on March 16, 1775. Botetourt freeholders addressed their statement to Andrew Lewis and John Bowyer, their chosen delegates to the upcoming Virginia Convention, but the identities of the men who drafted the document are unknown except for an acknowledgment that it was signed by "The Freeholders of Botetourt." The town of Fincastle, near present-day Roanoke, was in the eastern portion of Botetourt County and served as the county seat and the location of the county courthouse, so that is the most likely place where the freeholders met to draft their resolutions. In contrast, the Augusta County Resolutions published about one week later included a description of the freeholders' meeting, which had happened in late February at the courthouse in Staunton. Augusta's Resolutions were formatted much in the same way as the Botetourt's Resolutions with instructions issued to their delegates, Thomas Lewis and Samuel McDowell. However, Augusta also published the names of the group of men who drafted the instructions.[4]

The resolutions published by both Botetourt and Augusta included statements addressing the relationship between American colonists and Britain and a connection to their countrymen in other colonies. Demonstrating their deference to the crown, Botetourt County freeholders described

The able Doctor, or America Swallowing the Bitter Draught, 1777, engraving. The Miriam and Ira D. Wallach Division of Art, Prints, and Photographs: Print Collection, New York Public Library

"hearts replete with the most grateful and loyal veneration" for the House of Hanover, which had ruled Britain since the early 1700s, and their "dutiful affection for our Sovereign," while Augusta's described their "sentiments of loyalty and allegiance to his majesty king George" and "respect for the parent state." Both resolutions also went on to voice criticisms, with Botetourt declaring its contempt for the king's councilors whom it described as "a set of miscreants, unworthy to administer the laws of Britain's empire" and Augusta offering a slightly more subdued comment about settlers' unwillingness to "surrender . . . to any minister, to any parliament, or any body of men upon earth, by whom we are not represented, and in whose decisions therefore we have no voice." Augusta's freeholders noted that they were "determined to maintain unimpaired that liberty which is the gift of Heaven to the subjects of Britain's empire" and "join our countrymen in such measures as may be deemed wise and necessary to secure and perpetuate the ancient, just, and legal rights of this colony, and all British America."

Botetourt's freeholders explained that they wanted their statement published "[t]hat our countrymen, and the world, may know our disposition."[5]

Although both Botetourt and Augusta counties spanned adjacent swaths of western territory from the Blue Ridge Mountains to the Ohio River, the Botetourt Resolutions provide the clearest statement of an acute awareness of the settlers' situation on the western edge of Virginia and the feeling of unity across the American colonies. Referring to events in Boston that occurred more than a year earlier, the Botetourt freeholders stated that "the subjects of Britain are ONE; and when the honest man of Boston, who has broke no law, has his property wrested from him, the hunter on the Allegany must take the alarm." By expressing their support for the people of Boston, whose harbor was closed in 1774 as part of the Crown's reaction to the infamous tea party, Botetourt County freeholders joined, although belatedly, the public outcry against Britain cutting off Boston's trade activity. The animosity toward Britain across the American colonies continued to grow as legislatures and citizens expressed concern that what happened in Massachusetts could soon occur in their own communities.[6]

Perhaps most strikingly, the freeholders in both Botetourt and Augusta connected their commitment to liberty to Virginia's backcountry history. Augusta's freeholders noted that "[m]any of us and our forefathers left their native land, and explored this once savage wilderness, to enjoy the free exercise of the rights of conscience, and of human nature: These rights we are fully resolved with our lives and fortunes, inviolably to preserve." Botetourt's language was even more passionate with a statement of personal commitment that "my gun, my tomahawk, my life, I desire you to tender to the honour of my King and country." Botetourt's freeholders went on to directly address backcountry settlers' generational experiences with the statement that "my LIBERTY, to range these woods on the same terms my father has done is not mine to give up; it was not purchased by me, and purchased it was; it is entailed on my son, and the tenure is sacred . . . the original purchase was blood, and mine shall seal the surrender." With these expressions of the language of liberty connected to lived experience, the freeholders of Augusta and Botetourt made it clear that they had an equal interest in the outcomes of the political conversations taking place at the Virginia Conventions and the Continental Congress, but also that their support was personal and rooted in their individual and regional history of settlement.[7]

Botetourt County freeholders used their resolutions, as well as an additional statement directed to Virginia's delegates to the Continental Congress that was published in the *Virginia Gazette* on March 24, 1775, to express their appreciation and gratitude to their representatives. Botetourt's freeholders described Virginia's delegates to the First Continental Congress as "SONS of WORTH and FREEDOM," and pledged to "religiously observe their resolutions, and obey their instructions, in contempt of our power, and temporary interest." They described Virginia's delegates as "the guardians of our

Gentleman I allude to is Mr. Wallace.

To the Honourable Peyton Randolph, Richard Bland, Edmund Pendleton, Richard Henry Lee, Patrick Henry, George Waſhington, and Benjamin Harriſon, *Eſquires, Delegates from Virginia to the late General Congreſs.*

The ADDRESS *of the freeholders and inhabitants of the county of* Botetourt.

WE the freeholders and inhabitants of the county of Botetourt, aſſembled at the courthouſe, taking into our conſideration the unhappy diſputes which at preſent ſubſiſt between Great Britain and America, and being greatly alarmed at the dangerous and unconſtitutional meaſures adopted by Adminiſtration, with reſpect to the colonies, beg leave now to addreſs you as the guardians of our rights and privileges.

Pleaſe, therefore, to accept our moſt ſincere and grateful acknowledgments for your ſteady and patriotick conduct, in the ſupport of American liberty, at the late General Congreſs. And we aſſure you that although the alarming ſituation of our frontiers, for ſome time paſt, hath prevented our cooperating with our fellow ſubjects, in their laudable efforts to obtain redreſs of our common grievances, we highly approve of the plan you have adopted for that purpoſe, and ſhall moſt cheerfully abide by your reſolutions.

As you have ſo fully and clearly aſcertained the rights and liberties of American ſubjects, we have nothing to add on that head. We are happy to find our ſentiments entirely correſpond with yours, becauſe in theſe ſentiments we are determined to live and die.

We are too ſenſible of the ineſtimable privileges, enjoyed by ſubjects under the

"Address of the freeholders and inhabitants of the county of Botetourt," *Virginia Gazette*, March 24, 1775. VMHC

rights and privileges," noted that they "highly approve of the plan you have adopted," and were "happy to find our sentiments entirely correspond with yours, because in these sentiments we are determined to live and die." Echoing their earlier resolutions, they praised their privileges under the British constitution, loyalty to "our most gracious sovereign," and readiness to participate in "the defence of his person and government." Despite their praise, they concluded the statement with a call to action that "should a wicked and tyrannical Ministry, under the sanction of a venal and corrupt Parliament, persist in acts of injustice and violence towards us, they only must be answerable for the consequences. Liberty is so strongly impressed on our hearts, that we cannot think of parting with it but with our lives."[8]

The three published statements from Augusta and Botetourt counties in March 1775 are striking examples of backcountry settlers' sentiments on the cusp of the American Revolution and their perceptions of how they fit into Virginia and America's colonial landscape, as well as the British Empire. However, the language and emotion expressed in the resolutions cannot be fully understood unless it is situated within the broader context of the backcountry experience.

The Freeholders

Although minimal information is available about the authors and signers of these documents, it is important to consider their identities given the personal nature of the language they used in all three statements. Referring to their forefathers who explored and settled in the backcountry, their liberty "to range these woods on the same terms my father has done," the importance of passing this land-related liberty to their sons, and the "original purchase" in blood, these backcountry freeholders argued that claiming their lands had not simply been an issue of paper and pen, but one that required their sweat, their blood, and even their lives. For Augusta and Botetourt freeholders, their personal sacrifices cemented their land claims and gave them a greater reason to defend their homes against a local or distant foe.

It is impossible to uncover the identity of each freeholder from Augusta and Botetourt who was present for the meetings in their respective counties, but county records reveal the identities of some of the men who are likely to have been among the resolutions' authors and supporters based on their land holdings and demographics. County freeholders included the gentlemen justices and militia officers appointed by the county court, typically among the upper tiers of backcountry society, and individuals serving in various county roles like surveyor and sheriff. Though these positions existed in counties throughout Virginia, in the backcountry region these individuals were more likely to own hundreds of acres rather than thousands, live in a small frame house that might have been fortified in anticipation of Indian attacks, and cultivate diverse agriculture and livestock rather than the tobacco cash crop of eastern Virginia. In Augusta County there are at least forty men identified in the county order books who would have been freeholders. Botetourt County had at least twenty individuals identified in the county records who fulfilled the requirements for freeholders.[9]

Each county's resolution identified the two delegates who were to represent the county at the upcoming Virginia Convention. These four men—Thomas Lewis and Samuel McDowell for Augusta County, and Andrew Lewis and John Bowyer for Botetourt County—had similar backgrounds. Each one arrived in the Shenandoah Valley region alongside parents and siblings and had been in the area for several decades by the 1770s. Although Thomas Lewis and Andrew Lewis lived in separate counties in 1775, they were brothers from the well-known Lewis family. Both men had served as Augusta County justices before the creation of Botetourt County and while Thomas was Augusta's first surveyor, Andrew is best known for his military service in the French and Indian War and Dunmore's War. Samuel McDowell settled in the region with his parents decades earlier and his father died during an Indian attack along the James River. As an adult, Samuel served as a county official and led a militia company in Dunmore's War. John Bowyer had also been in the backcountry for several decades by 1775 and served as a captain in Augusta's militia before the creation of Botetourt County.[10]

Included in Augusta's Resolutions were also the names of the six men tasked with drafting the document: Alexander Balmain, Sampson Matthews, Alexander McClenachan, Michael Bowyer, William Lewis, and George Matthews. Among these men, Michael Bowyer was John

Bowyer's brother and William Lewis was brother to Thomas and Andrew. Some had military and militia service from the French and Indian War and Dunmore's War, and others, like brothers Sampson and George Matthews, were also well-established merchants and businessmen. While many of these men went on to greater prominence during the Revolutionary War, in 1775, except for Andrew Lewis, their prominence was primarily local as leaders in their counties and region. Except for Alexander Balmain, who was a recent arrival from Scotland, these individuals' and their families' long history in the backcountry means that they had been on the frontlines of the Indian Wars of the 1750s. Many had first moved into the region with their parents and had endured harrowing experiences of seeing death, violence, and even captivity as children. Examining the history behind the language used in Augusta and Botetourt counties' resolutions reveals the way those experiences shaped settlers' perspectives, actions, and evolving American identity as they paired that experience with Revolutionary-era rhetoric.[11]

Augusta and Botetourt before the Resolutions

When Virginia's House of Burgesses established Augusta County in 1738, it stretched "to the utmost limits of Virginia" at the edge of Britain's territorial claims, and as far south as the Virginia-North Carolina boundary. More than thirty years later, Botetourt County was carved out of this same expanse of backcountry land, so the histories of people and place were intertwined. Initially, the region's population was too small to support a county system of courts and local government, so it was not until 1745 that the court was organized with a courthouse constructed in what became Staunton, Virginia. Staunton is in the southern part of the Shenandoah Valley and the region was settled by an influx of Protestant Irish, known as the Scots-Irish today. As the county grew, eastern Augusta County, and the town of Staunton specifically, became an important hub on the Valley Road running through the Shenandoah Valley.[12]

The Indian Wars of the 1750s and 1760s greatly impacted the development of Augusta County as Virginia settlements intruded further west into Native American lands and exacerbated tensions. As a result of enduring conflict between Native Americans and Virginia settlers in eastern Augusta County, along the present-day Virginia-West Virginia state line, entire backcountry communities were often devastated or eliminated during times of war. One of the greatest periods of violence for Virginia's backcountry settlements came in the summer of 1755 with the failure of General Edward Braddock's western campaign to Fort Duquesne, the site of present-day Pittsburgh, Pennsylvania. Braddock's men were ambushed by French-allied Native Americans as they neared Fort Duquesne, Braddock himself was mortally wounded, and his army returned home in shambles. In the aftermath, the emboldened French allies among the Shawnee, the Mingo, and the Delaware

Shenandoah Valley, William Louis Sonntag, late 1850s, oil on canvas. VMHC, Purchased with funds provided by Lora M. Robins

A Plan of the Field of Battle and disposition of the Troops, as they were on the March at the time of the Attack on the 9.th of July 1755.

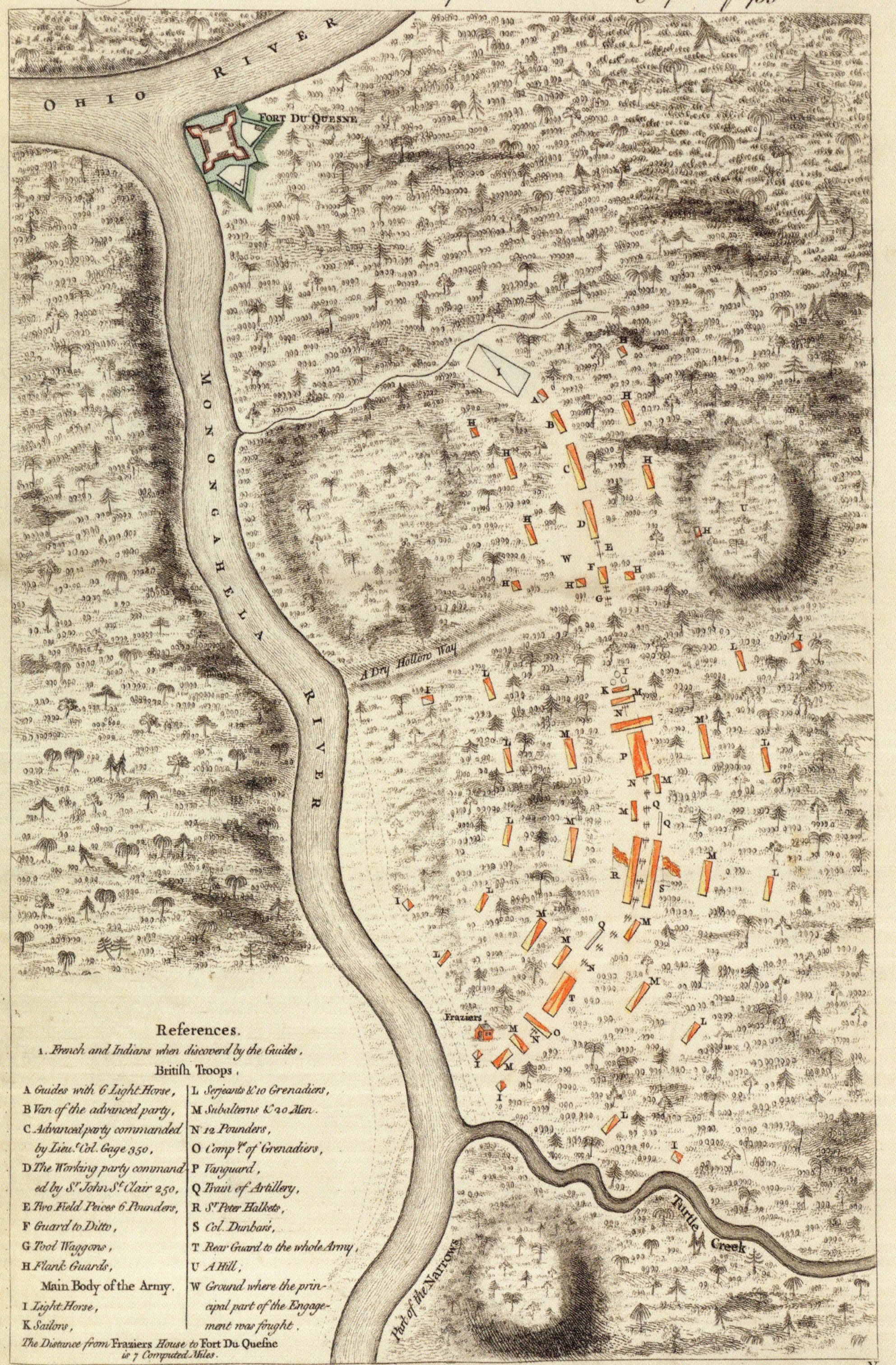

set out on a campaign throughout the backcountry of Pennsylvania, Maryland, and Virginia.[13]

The violence in Augusta County during the summer of 1755 included an Indian attack in the Greenbrier Valley near present-day Alderson, West Virginia, where, according to the *Virginia Gazette*, "Fifty Indians, supposed to be [Shawnees] . . . killed and captivated Fifteen People, burnt Eleven Houses, and drove off 500 Head of Cattle, Horses &c." The violence that summer also reached further east to the Draper's Meadow settlement, in present-day Blacksburg, where members of the prominent Draper and Ingles families and Augusta County official James Patton were killed. News of these attacks was far-reaching across Virginia and throughout the American colonies. In some western areas of Augusta, like the Greenbrier Valley, despite initially remaining on their lands after the 1755 attacks, settlers abandoned the region due to growing threats. These experiences were formative for the survivors.[14]

In the 1760s, backcountry settlers returned to the areas they had previously abandoned, unaware that they would soon experience another period of terror as part of Pontiac's War (1763–66). Though it was brief compared to the years of the French and Indian War, the violence associated with Pontiac's War resulted in tremendous loss of life, captivity, and the destruction of Virginia backcountry settlements. Pontiac, an Ottawa leader, attacked Fort Detroit in May 1763, and the violence reached the Virginia backcountry in July when more than fifty Shawnee led by Hokoleskwa, "the Cornstalk," principal chief of the Mequashake band of the Shawnee, attacked the Muddy Creek settlement in the Greenbrier Valley. This attack, often identified as the "Clendenin Massacre," devastated the Yocum, See, and Clendenin families among others in the community, with most of the men killed and many of the women and children taken into captivity. In the aftermath of these hostilities, the 1763 Proclamation established a boundary for settlement along the Eastern Continental Divide that effectively halted settlers from moving into the Allegheny Mountains. The treaties of Fort Stanwix and Hard Labor in 1768, aided by subsequent surveying and on-the-ground negotiations, encouraged backcountry settlers to press west with their families again, even if they were unable to secure titles to their land claims.[15]

New settlement warranted the formation of a new county and on November 23, 1769, the *Virginia Gazette* published the news that "[t]he petition for dividing the county of Augusta is agreed to by the House of Burgesses, and we hear the new county is to be named BOTETOURT," after Virginia's current royal governor, the well-loved Lord Botetourt, Norborne Berkeley, who had helped to restore settlement. The act establishing Botetourt County described the boundaries for the new county. A line was drawn from the South Mountain in the Shenandoah Valley to the west, dividing Augusta into two counties and parishes. The line was marked by trees bearing "AC" or "BC" on the appropriate sides of the line as it moved west across the Cowpasture River, Jackson's River, and over

Plans Showing the Braddock Expedition and Defeat in the Campaign Against Fort Duquesne, 1755, Robert Orme, 1758. VMHC, Bequest of Paul Mellon

The Right Honble Norborne Berkeley, Baron de Bottetourt, late Governor of Virginia, H. Ashby, 1774, sepia stipple engraving. The Colonial Williamsburg Foundation, Museum Purchase

WILLIAMSBURG, *November* 23.

We are informed, by a Gentleman from North-Carolina, that on the 7th inſtant his Excellency William Tryon, Eſq; Governor of that province, diſſolved the Aſſembly thereof, which had adopted the plan of the ſpirited reſolves of the patriotic and loyal Houſe of Burgeſſes of Virginia.

On Wedneſday the 1ſt inſtant (being the day on which the inhabitants of New-York nobly determined not to ſurrender their rights to arbitrary power) the Sons of Liberty aſſembled at Mr. De La Montayne's, and celebrated the ſame; when, among many other toaſts, the following were drank, viz.

"The patriotic HOUSE of BURGESSES of the dominion of VIRGINIA.

"The COUNCIL of VIRGINIA.

"The Printers who nobly diſregarded the deteſtable ſtamp-act, preferring the public good to their private intereſt, in 1765."

The petition for dividing the county of Auguſta is agreed to by the Houſe of Burgeſſes, and we hear the new county is to be named BOTETOURT.

The Katie, Clark, the Molly, Barron, the Cuninghame, Wylie, and the Molly, Scott, all from Glaſgow, are arrived in James river.

Capt. Barron ſpoke the Dutcheſs of Gordon, from London, for New-York, on the 12th inſtant, about 20 leagues E. from Cape Henry, out 6 weeks, all well.

"The petition for dividing the county of Augusta is agreed to by the House of Burgesses, and we hear the new county is to be named BOTETOURT," *Virginia Gazette*, November 23, 1769. VMHC

"the west side of Anthonys Creek Mountain which divides the Eastern & Western Waters" and down into the Greenbrier Valley before extending farther to the west.[16]

Anticipating future new western counties, the House of Burgesses recognized that many settlers would find travel to Botetourt's courthouse in the town of Fincastle challenging or even impossible, and the act stated that the county would likely be divided as soon as the population increased because "the people situated on the waters of the Mississippi, in the said county of Botetourt, will be very remote from their court-house." Botetourt County itself was divided just a few years later in 1772 along an east-west axis that followed the path of the New River and Kanawha River with the southern section becoming Fincastle County, while the town of Fincastle remained the seat of Botetourt County.[17]

Through the early 1770s, settlements along the Greenbrier River traversing both Augusta and Botetourt counties flourished. The uncertainty of the previous decades faded, and settlers lived without a major threat of warfare for several years. Family connections had always formed the backbone

of backcountry settlement, which often resulted in the destruction of entire families during conflicts with Indigenous peoples. However, in the Greenbrier Valley of the early 1770s, communities continued to grow out of extended family and kinship networks. Although the county seats of Augusta and Botetourt remained in the eastern portions of the counties near the Blue Ridge Mountains, the few settlements that had tentatively spread into the Appalachian Mountains in the 1760s consisted of more than a dozen communities across a geographic region spanning roughly 3,000 square miles and nearly two million acres around the Greenbrier Valley by 1773.[18]

Dunmore's War

By 1774, Augusta and Botetourt counties were well established with growing populations inching westward. But far-flung conflicts over land on the Ohio River and around Pittsburgh, Pennsylvania, as well as retributive actions between Native Americans and settlers in the Ohio Valley led to escalating tensions in the backcountry. Despite the distance between the Ohio Valley and settlements in Augusta and Botetourt, the settlers in those counties were on the frontlines of Virginia's western settlements and would be pulled into what was ultimately an offensive battle against the Shawnee, who were still led by Hokoleskwa, in response to those distant tensions.[19]

Southern American Long Rifle, about 1770–80. The Colonial Williamsburg Foundation, Museum Purchase

Among the men leading the county militias were future delegates and signers of both Augusta County and Botetourt County's 1775 resolutions, like Samuel McDowell, John Bowyer, brothers Sampson and George Matthews, and, of course, Andrew Lewis, who commanded this southern branch of the army. Other men included storekeeper John Stuart and Robert McClenachan from the Greenbrier Valley, and some whose names are still prominent in western Virginia like William Christian, the namesake of Christiansburg, and his brother-in-law William Campbell, as well as William Fleming, who was a veteran of the French and Indian War and a local physician. Approximately 1,000 men from the militias of Augusta, Botetourt, and Fincastle, and independent companies from Bedford, Dunmore, and Culpeper met at an area of Botetourt County along the Greenbrier River, now Lewisburg, West Virginia, designated as "Camp Union."[20]

Once the journey from Camp Union to the Native American towns near the Ohio River was underway, it was several weeks of trailblazing through about 160 miles of what John Stuart described as a "mountainous and rugged" route across Virginia's Appalachian Plateau. The first group of men from Augusta and Botetourt left the rendezvous point on September 6 and followed the Greenbrier River to the New River, then headed west across Gauley Mountain before winding along the Kanawha River, crossing the Gauley and Elk rivers, and finally reaching the forks of the Ohio. A month later there were still men spread across the route and some still just beginning their journey from Camp Union.[21]

According to an account published in the *Virginia Gazette*, on October 10, 1774, just before sunrise, two men discovered a group of Native Americans camped within a few miles of Lewis's army on the banks of the Ohio River and the battle soon began. The fierce clashes between the two sides continued throughout the day, with men taking cover and shooting from behind trees and brush. The sun was setting when the Virginians finally dislodged the Indians from the steep banks and tree cover and forced them to retreat across the Ohio River, carrying off their dead and wounded as they went. Once the battle ended, the Virginians had to care for their own wounded comrades. Isaac Shelby wrote that the "groans of our wound[ed] men lying around was Enough to shuder the stoutest hart." In the aftermath, those who were uninjured began construction on a fort to house the sick and wounded, collected the plunder strewn about the battlefield, gathered the cattle that had been left to wander during the battle, and buried the dead.[22]

William Fleming was the most well-known among the injured men, and his wounds were so severe that rumors of his death circulated in the *Virginia Gazette* alongside the first accounts of the battle. William Christian reported that Fleming was hit three times then stepped away "with great coolness and deliberation" and told his men "not to mind him but to go up and fight." Fleming, who was also a surgeon, wrote about his wounds and broken bones along with seeing his lungs "forced through the wound in my breast," but assured his wife in a letter that he "did not fall and had strength with Assistance to reach my tent."[23]

In addition to the physical labor of building a fort, burying the dead, caring for the wounded, and gathering more provisions, the men also faced the reality of reorganizing their companies and appointing officers to replace those who died. John Todd took over William Fleming's orderly book as Fleming's injuries prevented him from writing. There, Todd listed several men who succeeded their fallen leaders and included an address from Andrew Lewis to the Augusta troops about the loss of Colonel Charles Lewis, Andrew's youngest brother, who was the highly respected and admired commander of the Augusta militia. Todd wrote that Andrew Lewis addressed the troops, saying, "The Augusta line & I have too much reason to condole with one another. You have lost your brave leader & I in him have lost the best of Brothers." William Christian reported that when Charles Lewis was shot, "[h]e turned and handed his gun to a man and retired to camp, telling the men as he passed along 'I am wounded but go . . . and be brave.'"[24]

Just a few days after the battle, Lewis received instructions from Lord Dunmore to prepare to cross the Ohio River and travel to the Indian towns for a final confrontation. Andrew Lewis left a garrison of 300 men at the newly constructed fort at Point Pleasant and marched toward the Shawnee towns on the Scioto River. While en route, Lewis received word that Lord Dunmore had secured peace with the Shawnee, although it did not include the Cherokee or the Mingo. According to a letter from Lord Dunmore to the Earl of Dartmouth, the terms of peace required the Shawnee to deliver any prisoners to the Virginians, restore any valuables and horses they had captured, and agree to trade by the King's instructions. Most importantly for Virginia's backcountry settlers, the Shawnee agreed not to hunt south of the Ohio River "nor molest any Boats passing thereupon." Joseph Doddridge, a contemporary who wrote about Dunmore's War, presented a more emotional account, stating that despite establishing peace, "[i]t was with the greatest reluctance and chagrin" that Andrew Lewis's troops withdrew from the Ohio Country. The widespread violence and loss of "their relatives and friends at the big Levels and muddy Creek, and above all, their recent loss [of life] at the battle of the Point had inspired these big knives, as the Indians called the Virginians, with an inveterate thirst for revenge." The Virginians hoped destroying the Indian towns along the Scioto River would quench that thirst, but obeyed Lord Dunmore's order "with every expression of regret and disappointment."[25]

Although the battle of Point Pleasant was a victory for the Virginians, backcountry settlers still had to cope with the tremendous loss of life. William Christian reported from the battlefield that the "cries of the wounded prevented our resting" the night after the battle and that many who lingered would die as "[t]here are many shot in two places, one in particular I observed with two bullits, some in three." According to several contemporary accounts, among the Virginians there were approximately fifty killed and eighty to ninety men wounded in the battle. Native American losses are unknown as they were carried away from the battlefield. The impact of the Virginians' casualties was significant, considering how tightly knit backcountry communities who lost family and friends, leaders, businessmen, and tradespeople were. The number of men wounded at Point Pleasant was significant enough that in July 1775, the Third Virginia Convention appointed a committee to settle the public claims, examine the wounded, and allocate pensions for their relief.[26]

Blue Ridge Revolutionaries

Dunmore's War brought men from Augusta County and Botetourt County alongside others from Virginia's southern backcountry. Though many had experienced periods of backcountry violence and conflict, the fresh experience of warfare bound the men together as they struggled through time away from home and family, long marches and camp life, the emotions of victory, and the deaths of comrades, friends, and relatives.

After Lord Dunmore returned to Williamsburg in December of 1774, he submitted a report of his observations and concerns about backcountry settlers to the Earl of Dartmouth. Unknowingly hinting at what was to come, he described backcountry residents as a people who, in his view, did not fit within the behavioral norms of Englishmen. He wrote about backcountry inhabitants who were "impressed from their earliest infancy with Sentiments and habits,

About the year 1749 a person who was a Citizen of the County of
Frederick & subject to paroxisms of lunacy, when influenced by such
fits, usually made excursions into the Wilderness, & in his rambles
westwardly fell in on the waters of Greenbrier River, at that Time the
Country on the Western waters were but little known to the english
Inhabitants of the then Colonies of America being claimed by the French
who had commenced Settlements on the Ohio and its Waters west of the
Allegheny Mountains. The lunatic being surprised to find waters running a different course from any he had before known, returned with
the intelligence of his discovery which did abound with Game, this soon
excited the enterprize of others. Two men from New England of the name of
of Jacob Marlin & Stephen Sewel took up a residence in Greenbrier [illegible]
but soon disagreeing in Sentiment, a quarrel occasioned their seperation
& Sewel for sake of peace quit their Cabin & made his abode in a large
hollow tree, in this situation they were found by the late Genl Andrew
Lewis, in the year 1751 Mr Lewis was appointed Agent for a Company of
Grantees who obtained from the Governor & Council of Virginia an order
for 100.000 acres of land lying on the waters of Greenbrier River & pro-
ceed to make Surveys to complete the quantity of s'd granted land. Upon
[illegible] Marlin & Sewel, living in the Neighborhood of each other, enquired
what could induce them to live seperate in a wilderness so distant from
the habitations of any other human beings, they informed him that difference of opinions occasioned their seperation, and that they had since
enjoyed more tranquility and a better understanding; for Sewel said
that each morning when they arose & Marlin came out of the great house
& he from his hollow tree, they saluted each other, saying, "good morning
Mr Marlin, & good morning Mr Sewel" so that a good understanding
then existed between them, but it did not last, for Sewel removed about
forty miles farther West to a Creek that still bears his name there the
Indians found him and killed him. —

Previous to the year 1755 Mr Lewis had completed for
the Grantees under the order of Council upwards of 80.000 acres and
the war then commencing between England & France nothing farther
was done on the Business until the year 1761 when his Majesty's procl-

"Transcript of the memoir of Indian wars and other occurances, 1749–1780," John Stuart, copy made by Samuel Lewis about 1800. VMHC

very different from those acquired by persons of a Similar condition in England" and "do not conceive that Government has any right to forbid their taking possession of a Vast tract of Country." Although backcountry settlers supported Lord Dunmore at Point Pleasant for a mutually beneficial outcome, these distinctly American sentiments and habits became even more obvious in 1775 when Virginians' loyalty to the royal governor completely disintegrated.[27]

At a time when discourse necessitated action, the freeholders of Augusta and Botetourt counties enthusiastically joined the chorus of resolutions of support for the American cause and for their delegates ahead of the March 1775 Virginia Convention by drafting and publishing resolutions in the *Virginia Gazette*. As they pledged physical action to the cause, not only the generational experience of conflict but also the fresh emotion of warfare and loss was apparent in the language they chose.

When words became actions in 1775 and the realities of war continued through the 1780s, maintaining the level of enthusiasm expressed in Augusta and Botetourt counties' resolutions proved unsustainable, especially with battlefields often far from home. Virginia's backcountry inhabitants were willing to fight when the war came to their doorstep or region, but the "sentiments and habits" that Lord Dunmore observed were also evident in settlers' lack of interest in military service that required them to leave their homes and families, particularly as the backcountry continued to be an unstable geopolitical region prone to conflict. Despite a reluctance to join in the fray on someone else's terms, backcountry settlers lived among the sacrifices of the previous generations, faced the tenuousness of their own livelihoods, and looked to the promise of a future where they could be "happy, virtuous, and free" as they embraced an identity as Virginians and Americans.

Chapter 3

Religious Liberty and Revolution in Virginia

Alan Taylor

Before the American Revolution, Virginia was a land of glaring and accepted inequality. A visitor from England noted, "There is a greater distinction supported between the different classes of life here, than perhaps in any of the rest of the colonies." Enslaved people suffered the most at the bottom of society, but common whites also felt dominated by the top 2 percent of the people who were wealthy and genteel planters and who held the top political positions. A plain Virginian, Devereux Jarratt, recalled the awe he felt when in the presence of the colonial elite: "We were accustomed to look upon, what were called *gentle folks*, as beings of a superior order. For my part, I was quite shy of *them*, and kept off at a humble distance."[1]

Born in New Kent County in 1733, Jarratt grew up in a family of middling means. His parents owned a substantial farm, but they lacked formal education and held no enslaved people. He remembered, "They always had plenty of plain food and raiment, wholesome and good [and] suitable to their humble station, and the times in which they lived." The Jarratts expected their children to remain in the same class: "My parents neither sought nor expected any titles, honors, or great things, either for themselves or children." Aspiration to wealthy gentility seemed foolish. Instead, the Jarratts feared falling into poverty, which middling folk fended off by educating their children. In a rural neighborhood, middling-class parents hired a teacher to conduct a seasonal, winter school, which offered a rudimentary education. Jarratt noted, "Their highest ambition was to teach their children to read, write, and understand the fundamental rules of arithmetic. . . . Philosophy, Rhetoric, Logic, &c., we never heard of."[2]

Jarratt learned to work as a farmer and carpenter, but he felt drawn to studying theology. Aspiring to the ministry, Jarratt sought to straddle the cultural divide emerging in mid-century Virginia, between the established Anglican church favored by the gentry and the rising and more populist evangelical movement. Evangelicals appealed to souls troubled by the world and longing for a heavenly respite after death. Preachers cultivated in listeners a painful despair until it ripened into an emotional release, known as the New Birth, a feeling of blissful union

James Madison (detail), Thomas Sully, after the original by Gilbert Stuart, 1856, oil on canvas. VMHC, Gift of Jaquelin Plummer Taylor

with God. Evangelicals demanded a strict new code of behavior, renouncing the worldly pleasures of Anglican gentry and parsons as soul-destroying distractions from the pursuit of eternal salvation. An Anglican teacher complained that dissenters were "destroying pleasure in the Country; for they encourage ardent Pray'r; strong & constant faith, & an intire Banishment of *Gaming*, *Dancing*, & Sabbath-Day Diversions." Joining an evangelical church meant submitting to moral supervision by new brethren and sisters.[3]

Initially, Virginia's evangelicals came from the lower and middling ranks of society, for the gentry identified the cultural upheaval as destabilizing to social order. Magistrates arrested, jailed, and fined preachers while mobs broke up their meetings and flogged some leading evangelicals. By shaking off jailing and whipping, evangelicals demonstrated their zeal and impressed others, which, by the 1770s, led the gentry to suspend further persecution. When resistance to British taxes ripened into revolution against British rule, the gentry had to confront the place of religion in an independent state. Could that state continue to support a single denomination as a unique source of cohesion and order? Or would the state embark on a radical experiment in allowing individuals to choose their faith and fund only their preferred ministers?[4]

Choices

In the culture war of eighteenth-century Virginia, Devereux Jarratt felt conflicted. Although he coveted the privileges and prestige of the Anglican ministry, his humble roots drew him to the more plebian and emotional style of evangelical preachers. His ideal was the great English evangelist George Whitefield who had toured the colonies, thrilling enormous crowds with fiery and theatrical preaching. Despite his controversial style, Whitefield clung to the established church and elite patrons—as did Jarratt.[5]

Ordained as an Anglican minister in 1763, Jarratt obtained a parish in Dinwiddie County. As the cultural divide widened in Virginia, Jarratt battled both sides. Drawn to the forceful, spontaneous style of evangelical preaching, he faulted his Anglican peers as dull and uninspired by God. Jarratt alleged that a typical parson preached "wholly by a written copy [and] he kept his eyes continually fixed on the paper" so that "what he said seemed rather addrest to the cushion, than to the congregation." Jarratt concluded that Anglicans delivered "smooth harrangues, in no wise calculated to disturb their carnal repose, or awaken any one to a sense of guilt and danger." But he sought to reform the established church from within rather than break away to join the Baptists or Methodists, who could not afford a professional ministry.[6]

By colonial law, every parish collected taxes on all property owners to sustain the Anglican church favored by the distant king and the local gentry. That church establishment discouraged religious dissenters from rival denominations as reckless dividers of community harmony. In 1751, five Anglican parsons praised the "Glory of this Colony, which hitherto hath

George Whitefield, M.A.,
Elisha Gallaudet, frontispiece
from *Memoirs of the Life of the Reverend George Whitefield, M.A.*,
by the Rev. John Gillies, 1774,
engraving. Library of Congress

8. That all power of ſuſpending laws, or the execution of laws, by any authority without conſent of the repreſentatives of the people, is injurious to their rights, and ought not to be exerciſed.

9. That laws having retroſpect to crimes, and puniſhing offences, committed before the exiſtence of ſuch laws, are generally oppreſſive, and ought to be avoided.

10. That in all capital or criminal proſecutions a man hath a right to demand the cauſe and nature of his accuſation, to be confronted with the accuſers or witneſſes, to call for evidence in his favour, and to a ſpeedy trial by an impartial jury of his vicinage, without whoſe unanimous conſent he cannot be found guilty, nor can he be compelled to give evidence againſt himſelf; that no man be deprived of his liberty except by the law of the land, or the judgment of his peers.

11. That exceſſive bail ought not to be required, nor exceſſive fines impoſed, nor cruel and unuſual puniſhments inflicted.

12. That warrants unſupported by evidence, whereby any officer or meſſenger may be commanded or required to ſearch ſuſpected places, or to ſeize any perſon or perſons, his or their property, not particularly deſcribed, are grievous and oppreſſive, and ought not to be granted.

13. That in controverſies reſpecting property, and in ſuits between man and man, the ancient trial by jury is preferable to any other, and ought to be held ſacred.

14. That the freedom of the preſs is one of the great bulwarks of liberty, and can never be reſtrained but by deſpotick governments.

15. That a well regulated militia, compoſed of the body of the people, trained to arms, is the proper, natural, and ſafe defence of a free ſtate; that ſtanding armies, in time of peace, ſhould be avoided, as dangerous to liberty; and that, in all caſes, the military ſhould be under ſtrict ſubordination to, and governed by, the civil power.

16. That the people have a right to uniform government; and therefore, that no government ſeparate from, or independent of, the government of *Virginia*, ought, of right, to be erected or eſtabliſhed within the limits thereof.

17. That no free government, or the bleſſing of liberty, can be preſerved to any people but by a firm adherence to juſtice, moderation, temperance, frugality, and virtue, and by frequent recurrence to fundamental principles.

18. That religion, or the duty which we owe to our CREATOR, and the manner of diſcharging it, can be directed only by reaſon and conviction, not by force or violence; and therefore, that all men ſhould enjoy the fulleſt toleration in the exerciſe of religion, according to the dictates of conſcience, unpuniſhed and unreſtrained by the magiſtrate, unleſs, under colour of religion, any man diſturb the peace, the happineſs, or ſafety of ſociety. And that it is the mutual duty of all to practice Chriſtian forbearance, love, and charity, towards each other.

Printed draft of the first proposed form of the Virginia Declaration of Rights, printed by Alexander Purdie, 1776. VMHC

been remarkably happy for uniformity of Religion." Virginia's colonial leaders insisted that religious uniformity promoted a Christian morality that sustained law and order and obedience to political authority. Without such cohesion, gentry and parsons imagined society collapsing into a grim and violent anarchy of unrestrained self-assertion.[7]

The establishment was expensive. Each parish sustained a substantial brick church and provided the minister with a farm (known as a "glebe") and a salary set at 16,000 pounds of tobacco, which the minister then sold for cash or credit. At an average of thirty-five pounds of tobacco per taxpayer, the parish levy was twice as high as any other tax paid in a Virginia county.[8]

That expensive establishment offended the growing number of evangelicals, who resented having to pay taxes for a clergy whom they did not respect. Asserting the right of each person to choose his or her own faith, evangelicals challenged the overlap of church, state, and society so dear to gentry and parsons. Itinerant evangelical ministers defied Virginia law, which demanded that they obtain a license and preach in no more than one county. During the mid-eighteenth century, magistrates arrested, jailed, and fined preachers or encouraged common mobs to disrupt evangelical meetings, sometimes flogging or dunking preachers. Their persistence through pain impressed common people, winning converts. By the 1770s, many gentry balked at further persecution as pointless. In addition, most leading Virginians felt preoccupied with the clash with Britain—and they sought to unite their constituents for that struggle.[9]

To win a difficult revolutionary war against a powerful empire, Virginia's Patriot leaders needed popular support. They had to have the backing of common men, serving as soldiers, jurors, voters, and taxpayers. To appeal to them, Patriot leaders challenged the traditional, colonial notion of society as a hierarchy of inequality stretching downward from the king through the gentry and middle class to laborers, servants, and enslaved Virginians at the bottom. Instead, Patriots championed a society imagined as composed of freely contracting and autonomous individuals, each with the same rights (except for enslaved people).[10]

Deriding inherited advantages as artificial and unjust, Patriots sought to substitute a more "natural" social order led by worthy men chosen by a broad electorate of white men. To recruit popular support for the Revolution, Patriot leaders promised equal legal and political rights for free men. The Revolution enticed ambitious common men with access to increased leadership positions as militia officers, county committeemen, and legislators. The Patriots also cut the poll tax, the colony's most regressive levy on white men.[11]

By championing individual liberty, Patriots shifted the culture war in favor of evangelicals who had long promoted free choice in religion. Delighted by the shift, evangelicals posed as the truest supporters of the new republic. In Albemarle County, a Baptist elder preached that "he knew of no difference between his patriotism and his religion." Formerly seen as a threat to the social hierarchy of colonial Virginia, evangelicals championed the new social order premised on equal rights for free white men.[12]

Patriot leaders wooed common men by liberating them from the burdens and responsibilities of supporting an established church. Of course, evangelicals welcomed that liberation—but so did many impious Virginians who just wanted to keep more money in their pockets. In June 1776, the state's new Declaration of Rights guaranteed the "free exercise of religion, according to the dictates of conscience." In a key step, Patriots redefined freedom of conscience as a natural and inalienable right of individuals rather than a concession granted by the legislature. Therefore, no magistrate could violate any man's conscience by forcing him to attend or support another church. In December 1776, the legislature suspended tax support for Anglican ministers—and permanently banned that support three years later. Devereux Jarratt bitterly recalled "when the republican assembly took away my living, in the year 1776, by . . . a stroke of power; and thereby subjected me to the caprice of the multitude."[13]

Mortifications

During the war, Anglican parsonages and churches suffered from vandalism by common Patriots who claimed to smite symbols of royal domination. When parsons retired or moved away, most parishes were too poor to replace them. As pulpits became empty, the outflow of parishioners to evangelical churches or rowdy taverns became a flood. Common folk preferred either more whiskey or the cheaper ministry of Baptist preachers, who made do with modest contributions while tending their own small farms. Losing his parishioners, Devereux Jarratt mourned: "When I now go to places, where formerly some hundreds used to attend my sermons, I can scarcely get forty hearers." Most of his former adherents embraced the Baptists: "I have the mortification to behold those, who were once my near and dear friends, yea my children in the gospel, fall off from me, and join with my most notorious enemies." By 1790, Baptists had surged to become the state's largest single denomination, with 204 churches and 262 ministers.[14]

To compensate for lost tax support, Anglican ministers relied on subscriptions by vestrymen and other leading parishioners. But too many subscribers failed to pay. As more laymen defected to evangelical meetings or lapsed into irreligion, the remaining subscribers balked at their growing burden to support a dying church. Jarratt dared not sue the many defaulters on his subscription because "it is made a pretext to confirm the popular cry—that money is all and all with me." Another parson lamented that ministers received little in a society where "every man [is] at liberty to contribute or not to the support of the Minister of his own persuasion as he judges best." Parsons felt betrayed by their laity, who still expected religious services without paying much for them.[15]

Once the war was over and won, the remaining parsons and their supporters hoped for a retreat from egalitarian individualism in favor of a renewed communal commitment to religion. To help that cause, in 1784 they

James Madison, Thomas Sully, after the original by Gilbert Stuart, 1856, oil on canvas. VMHC, Gift of Jaquelin Plummer Taylor

severed their ties to Britain and rebranded as the Episcopal Church in Virginia. But that church could only prosper, one parson predicted, if legislators again "thought public religion essential not only to the good order but to the very existence of government. . . . Otherwise, they cannot reasonably expect that religion will flourish in a country where its ministers are reduced to a state of beggary and contempt." Episcopalians subscribed to a Gresham's law of religion: that cheap preaching drove out the good as ignorant people preferred "the harangues of fanaticks" rather than the "sensible discourses of sober-minded rational men." Episcopalians insisted that public morality was a public good, which required tax support for community worship. Without publicly funded religion, they alleged, society would collapse into a vicious, selfish anarchy.[16]

Assessments

Rather than revive their old establishment, Episcopalians sought a general-assessment tax to support ministers of all denominations. A general assessment would tax every landholder but allow him to choose the church that should receive his payment, or else he could designate his payment to support a school. In 1784, legislative supporters insisted that the tax would promote "a general diffusion of Christian *knowledge* . . . to correct the morals of men, restrain their vices, and preserve the peace of society." The proposed bill would amend the voluntary principles of the new order by denying the most common choice made by Virginians: to avoid taxes and support no church and no school.[17]

Baptists denounced general assessment as reuniting church and state, thereby violating Virginia's Declaration of Rights. Evangelicals regarded any relationship between church and state as mutually corrosive. Baptists insisted that ministers should answer only to their brethren and Jesus. With Episcopalians supporting a general assessment, and Baptists opposing, Presbyterians became the swing element in the politics of religion. Disappointed by voluntary contributions, their clergymen found a general assessment tempting. In the fall of 1784, they tentatively endorsed the proposed tax. But those ministers did not bargain on their lay people, who bitterly opposed any cooperation with the Episcopalians. During the summer of 1785, the Presbyterian clergy beat a hasty retreat, unanimously revoking support for general assessment.[18]

That Presbyterian shift and a general distaste for paying taxes swung the political tide in the legislature. Deeply in debt to British merchants, planters struggled to pay taxes during the mid-1780s, when a commercial depression decreased the demand for, and price of, tobacco. In 1785–86, petitions to the legislature ran twelve-to-one against general assessment. A wry legislator declared, "We are all contending for popular applause & he is the cleverest fellow who bellows most against taxes" as "distressing the good citizens of the country, who are so dear to us all."[19]

The legislative supporters of assessment gave up, and their chief opponent, James Madison, seized the initiative by reviving a "Statute for Religious Freedom" first proposed by Thomas Jefferson in 1779 but postponed then. Weary of political agitation over religion and eager to consolidate the Revolution, the legislators overwhelmingly passed the statute (74 to 20) in January 1786. The statute banned state assistance to any church. A year later, the next legislature repealed the act incorporating the Episcopal Church in Virginia, thereby dissolving Virginia's long and special relationship with the Episcopal Church.[20]

Glebes

However, there was one last battle line: over the church buildings and farm glebes paid for by colonial taxpayers and retained by Episcopalians. Envious evangelicals cast that property as the ill-gotten gains of a corrupt establishment, which had duped and exploited the common people of colonial Virginia. In impassioned petitions to the legislature, Baptists denounced the glebes as the bastard offspring of "the adulterous connection between Church and State, the impositions of king craft and priest craft." Bitter memories of past persecution endured in the politics of religion after the Revolution.[21]

Episcopalians defended the glebes and churches as private property, which the state could not confiscate with any pretense to justice. Citing their sacrifices to sustain a united front during the Revolution, Episcopalians recited the legislative pledge of 1776, reserving their church property "in all time coming." Former persecutors, Episcopalians now felt persecuted.[22]

During the late 1780s and early 1790s, legislators defeated motions to confiscate the glebes but did so by dwindling margins. At last, in January 1798, the legislative dam gave way. By a 99 to 52 vote, the House of Delegates authorized counties to confiscate. The state senate held out for another year before caving in January 1799. The law declared that all Anglican property had "devolved on the good people of this commonwealth on the dissolution of the British government here." In January 1802, legislators passed an act that authorized county overseers of the poor to sell all glebes not currently occupied by an Episcopal minister. A county could confiscate the remaining glebes once the incumbent ministers left or died.[23]

Defeated in the legislature, Episcopalians appealed to the courts to strike down the confiscatory laws as unconstitutional. In 1803, the key test case reached the state court of appeals. The plaintiffs cast the glebes as a private property retained by a church, which had continued from the colonial into the republican era. The defendants of confiscation countered that the Revolution was a radical disjuncture that had vested the church's property in the republican state. The attorney general insisted "that all the rights which the church ever had, were overset by the *revolution* and nullified by the [state] *Bill of Rights*." The four justices split evenly, producing a deadlock that preserved a lower court ruling in support of confiscation.[24]

Losing the glebes accelerated the decline of the Episcopal Church, as they

Ruins of Jamestown, John Gadsby Chapman, 1834, oil on wood. VMHC

had been a chief means of recruiting and supporting clergymen. In 1775, the church had ninety-five active parishes. That number declined to forty-five by 1785 and took a further dive to twenty-five by 1805. During the 1810s, John Marshall was a devout Episcopalian as well as the chief justice of the United States. When asked to contribute money to educate young men for the clergy, Marshall sighed "that it was a hopeless undertaking, and that it was almost unkind

John Marshall, James Reid Lambdin, 1832, oil on canvas. VMHC, Purchased with funds provided by Hunton & Williams in honor of Justice Lewis F. Powell, Jr.

to induce young Virginians to enter the Episcopal ministry, the Church being too far gone ever to be revived."[25]

Most of the old parish churches crumbled from neglect and vandalism. A visitor found many "with the windows broken, and doors dropping off the hinges, and lying open to the pigs and cattle wandering about the woods." In Isle of Wight County, people pulled down the old Anglican church to build a kitchen from the bricks and reused the pews as stalls for a stable—until lightning struck to burn the whole. The people swapped the church bell for a still to make brandy, which better suited the tastes of post-Revolutionary Virginia. After the Revolution, the parish church no longer drew together local communities. Instead, people divided into rival churches or belonged to none. The choice had become their own—as had the tax savings.[26]

Colonial Virginia had sustained the largest and best-funded church establishment in British America, but after the Revolution the state adopted the strictest separation of church and state in the new nation. That separation terminated tax support for the Anglican church. By also taking the glebes, Virginia went far beyond any other state that dissolved its church establishment. Maryland, South Carolina, New York, and the New England states abolished church-state ties but left religious property alone. At an average of about 300 acres, multiplied by ninety-five parishes, the Virginia confiscations exceeded 25,000 acres.[27]

The move against the church establishment decisively shifted public finance in Virginia. Prior to the Revolution, the parish tax had been the greatest single tax levied on Virginians; its elimination cut the local tax burden by two-thirds. Poor relief suffered as the new county overseers spent less per capita than had the old vestries. After 1790, per capita taxes, paid by free men in Virginia, were only a third of those in Massachusetts. Thomas Jefferson had hoped that Virginians would reinvest their tax savings from disestablishment by funding a public system of education for white children. Instead, the state and county leaders decided to keep the money in their pockets and pose as champions of individual liberty.[28]

Individuals

The separation of church and state became white Virginians' proudest accomplishment in the American Revolution. In November 1824, the Marquis de Lafayette, a French veteran of the Revolution, returned to Virginia on a triumphant tour. Visiting his old friend James Madison, at his home of Montpelier, Lafayette urged his host and friends to do more to end slavery in Virginia. According to Lafayette's secretary, the hosts countered that Europe remained enslaved by "the religions of the state. The friends of Mr. Madison congratulated themselves that at least this species of slavery is unknown in the United States." The Virginians continued, "Religious liberty we possess in the full extent of its meaning. . . . Thanks to our new laws, worthy of the immortal legislators who were entrusted with framing them, no individual can be compelled to practice any religious worship, nor to frequent any place,

Thomas Jefferson, Louis Mathieu Didier Guillaume, after the original by Gilbert Stuart, 1858, oil on canvas. VMHC, Gift of Thomas Jefferson Randolph and George Wythe Randolph

nor to support any minister, of any religion whatever." They cast disestablishment as so grand that it gave them a pass for clinging to slavery.[29]

Older men struggled to adjust to the new, more competitive, individualistic, and contentious society of post-Revolutionary Virginia. White Virginians remained unequal in means but far more adept at dwelling on their equal rights. At elections, prosperous gentlemen won more offices than ever before, becoming congressmen and state representatives and senators, but they did so by proclaiming deference to the common voters. Those voters delighted in the praise, their lower taxes, the preservation of slavery, and the new freedom to choose a church or to attend none at all.[30]

The colonial gentry had frightened Devereux Jarratt as a boy, but he missed them when they were gone. "In our high *republican times*, there is more *levelling* than ought to be, consistent with good government. . . . At present, there is too little regard and reverence paid to magistrates and persons in public office," Jarratt sighed. He doubted that republicanism had improved Virginia: "An idea is held out to us, that our present government and laws are far superior to the former, when we were under the royal administration; but my age enables me to know, that the people are not now, by half, so quietly and peaceably governed as formerly; nor are the laws, perhaps by the tenth part, so well executed." Although he admired a republic in theory, Jarratt found it frustrating in practice. "This can arise from nothing so much as the want of a proper distinction, between the various orders of the people." In Jarratt's view, common people had become too pushy and crass, while the gentry were more irresponsible. Everyone seemed more selfish in the new age of individualism.[31]

Marquis de Lafayette, attributed to Ary Scheffer, about 1822, oil on canvas. National Portrait Gallery, Smithsonian Institution, Gift of the John Hay Whitney Collection

Chapter 4

The Picture of John Harris: A Story of Race, Orality, and Literacy in Revolutionary Virginia

Antonio T. Bly

Thomas Jefferson might have been mistaken in his estimation of the sheer numbers of enslaved people who joined the ranks of the British before the conclusion of America's struggle for independence when he wrote, "I supposed the state of Virginia lost under L[or]d. Cornwallis's hands that year [1781] about 30,000 slaves," but he did nonetheless capture an inkling about Black aspirations for their freedom. Before actual fighting broke out between Great Britain and her North American subjects, well over 1,000 Virginians of African descent in the tobacco colony declared themselves free of the tyranny of their Anglo-American oppressors. In the broad daylight, others pretended to be free. Using the stars as their guide, many more ran away—in the company of a loved one, a family member, a child, or even a fictive spouse. By the time Mr. Jefferson and his contemporaries officially declared their independence, that number of runaway slaves had grown considerably. Like the words enshrined in his inspiring and yet problematic Declaration of Independence, enslaved people in Virginia registered their grievance with the institution of slavery by forcing their masters to turn to print and the public at large for help. As Virginians grew tired of King George III's sovereignty over them, Black people in the colony were also weary of their enslavers. Like the sage of Monticello, they too believed that "all men are created equal." They too believed that they were entitled to their "unalienable Rights" to "life, liberty, and the pursuit of happiness." In increasing numbers, Virginians of African descent embraced the proposition of "Liberty or Death." Freedom, they thought, was worth fighting for.[1]

But even before Thomas Jefferson could record the deep-seated anxieties felt by

Music and Dance in Beaufort County (detail), attributed to John Rose, about 1785, watercolor on paper. The Colonial Williamsburg Foundation, Gift of Abby Aldrich Rockefeller

Table 1
Estimated Number of Runaway Slaves in Virginia, 1700–1799

Years	Captives Returned [a]	Fugitives Sought [b]	Captives Offered [c]	Fugitives Claimed [d]	Total
1700–1709	200	–	–	–	200
1710–1719	320	–	–	–	320
1720–1729	410	–	–	–	410
1730–1739	580	70	10	–	660
1740–1749	680	260	20	–	960
1750–1759	950	380	60	–	1,390
1760–1769	710	700	110	–	1,520
1770–1779	–	960	470	2,840	4,270
1780–1789	–	1,000	150	1,900	3,050
1790–1799	–	1,130	170	–	1,300
1700–1799	3,850	4,500	990	4,740	14,080

Notes: All figures have been rounded

a. Based on slaveowners' newspaper advertisements for their runaways in Virginia county courts and in the Houses of Burgesses.
b. Based on slaveowners' newspaper advertisements for their runaways.
c. Based on jailers' advertisements and occasional advertisements by individuals for captured runaways.
d. Based on claims submitted by individual slaveowners for slaves lost to the British and a list of evacuees who reported a Virginia residence.

Source:
Philip D. Morgan and Michael L. Nichols, "Slave Flight: Mount Vernon, Virginia, and the Wider Atlantic World," in Tamara Harvey and Greg O'Brien, eds., *George Washington's South* (Gainesville: University Press of Florida, 2004), 205.

many of his compatriots in Revolutionary Virginia, enslaved people were fermenting their own unique revolution. By protesting slavery with their feet, they made manifest the revolutionary fervor of the day. Well before 1776, in numerous court documents and newspaper advertisements that reported the actions and activities of fugitives, Black Virginians compelled their oppressors to publish their disapproval with them. Over the course of the eighteenth century, they not only took matters into their own hands, but also professed themselves independent of the despotism of history that tended to relegate them to the margins of colonial life. Even though they left few written records behind, enslaved Virginians brazenly snatched the intertwined laurels of history, authorship, and humanity away from their enslavers. By running away from those who had reduced them to enslavement, who were then forced to turn to print, they denounced what one former New England slave-poet described as that "modern Egyptian" bondage that had been their plight. Like the "Israelites" of the Old Testament, they were "impatient of Oppression." They longed for "Deliverance." They rejected the "strange Absurdity" of their enslavers whose "Conduct," that is whose "Words and Actions are so diametrically, opposite." In their bold bids to own themselves, they demonstrated that sacred "Principle," the "Love of Freedom," that "God has implanted" in "every human Breast." In notices printed on half sheets, their revolutionary stories are told—the stories of numerous freedom seekers who were dogged in their determination to be free, long before the idea of freedom became a part of the American creed.[2]

Although considerable attention has been given to the story of Black people participating in Revolutionary Virginia as either passive or active historical actors, or even as forced founders, less known is the story or stories of how they became aware of the burgeoning crisis between Great Britain and her North American colonies. Indeed, overlooked is the story of the ideological origins of the American Revolution among Black people, to borrow a phrase from the eminent historian Bernard Bailyn. Even though their revolution began well before the 1760s and 1770s, how did enslaved Virginians learn of the *other* American Revolution, the one that would transform thirteen British North American colonies into free and independent states? Where did they get their information about that struggle for independence? Though much has been made of the ways in which Black people in the Chesapeake participated in, and even influenced, the history of the Revolutionary era in the colony, little attention has been given to the subject of how they knew what they knew before they themselves elected to act on their own accord. Indeed, less known is the story of Black Virginians, like Johnny, the trusted slave of the Randolph family, who learned about the politically charged times in which he lived vis-à-vis the complex oral and literary culture that existed in the colony, and who would eventually choose to abscond during the upheaval brought by the Revolution.[3]

Within the context of the Black experience in Revolutionary Virginia,

Johnny's story is a multifaceted one. But like most stories about Black people who lived during the eighteenth century, his is one almost concealed by the very documents that shed some light on his life. Like most Black people, he did not write an autobiography. He did not keep a log of his life. Instead, he was the subject of writing. In other words, the peculiar institution of slavery had almost cut off fully those avenues to record the tragic story of his experience in the Chesapeake. Only through his actions and deeds did he manage to inscribe himself in print and therefore into the annals of history.

WILLIAMSBURG, *Dec.* 10, 1777.

I WILL *give a reward of five dollars, besides what the law allows, to any person who will apprehend* Johnny, *otherwise called* John Harris, *a mulatto man slave who formerly waited upon my uncle, the late* Peyton Randolph, *Esq; and secure him, so that I may get him again. He took with him, when he went away, a green broadcloth coat, and a new crimson waistcoat and breeches, a light coloured* Bath *coating great coat, a* London *brown* Bath *coating close bodied coat, a pair of old crimson cloth breeches, and some changes of clothes. He is about five feet seven or eight inches high, wears straight hair, cut in his neck, is much addicted to drinking, has gray eyes, can read and write tolerably well, and may probably endeavour to pass for a freeman. The above reward of five dollars will be given if he is taken in* Virginia, *but five pounds, besides what the law allows, will be paid to any person who apprehends him out of* Virginia, *and conveys him to me.*

EDMUND RANDOLPH.

Edmund Randolph's runaway notice concerning John Harris, *Virginia Gazette*, December 1, 1777. VMHC

During the early days of the tumultuous imperial crisis, the Black Virginian took matters into his own hands and decided to run away from his enslaver. His audacious act not only recorded a moment of resistance and agency, but also earned for the enslaved man the rare but intertwined laurels of history and authorship. Two days passed before Edmund Randolph, Johnny's enslaver, sent word to Alexander Purdie, who owned one of the four printing presses that operated in the colony. Amid notices for James Harrifield, who deserted from the "second *Georgia* battalion of continental troops," a "negro wench named *Daphne*," who absconded from Charles Burton's place in "*Sandy* creek," Pittsylvania, and an advertisement for a "black mare, and a two year old colt," recently taken up, the newspaperman published the story of Johnny's life in his *Virginia Gazette*. As the bulletin attests, Johnny played a central role in both the production and the publication of his slave narrative. For through his actions, the self-fashioned man inscribed in print the story of his life. It is an ironic and multilayered tale in which one rebelled against his owner who had thought himself a rebel, albeit in a different light.[4]

Edmund Randolph, John J. Reardon's biography of the prominent Virginian explains, considered himself a patriarch and a steadfast patriot. Perhaps best known for introducing the Virginia Plan to the Constitutional Convention of 1787, the Virginia gentleman found himself at odds with the bondservant he inherited from his uncle. Considering Johnny's familiarity with his surroundings, Randolph did not wait long before turning to his neighbors for help in securing the eloped bondservant. Unlike other subscribers who gave their eloped slaves time to return on their own, Randolph did not. In an era in which the social and political discord of the day had been becoming increasingly

Table 2
Intervening Periods Before Virginians Reported Fugitives Missing (Measured in Percentages)

Years	>1 month	1 month	2 months	3–5 months	6–12 months	<1 year	N/A
1730–1739	54	25	9	6	3	–	3
1740–1749	22	25	11	7	15	–	19
1750–1759	43	26	4	6	13	4	4
1760–1769	23	20	11	14	8	5	20
1770–1779	26	22	10	16	8	2	16

Sources:
Lathan A. Windley, *Runaway Slave Advertisements: A Documentary History* (4 vols.; Westport, Conn.: Greenwood Press, 1983); Billy G. Smith and Richard Wojtowicz, *Blacks Who Stole Themselves: Advertisements for Runaways in the Pennsylvania Gazette, 1728–1790* (Philadelphia: University of Pennsylvania Press, 1989); Graham Russell Gao Hodges and Alan Edward Brown, eds., *"Pretends to Be Free": Runaway Slave Advertisements from Colonial and Revolutionary New York and New Jersey* (New York: Fordham University, 1994); Antonio T. Bly, ed., *Escaping Bondage: A Documentary History of Runaway Slaves in Eighteenth-Century New England, 1700–1789* (Lanham, Md.: Lexington Books, 2012); *Readex: America's Historical Newspapers Database*; *Eighteenth-Century American Newspapers in the Library of Congress in Microfilm*.

commonplace, the Williamsburg grandee thought waiting might embolden the fugitive. After all, the mulatto man did challenge his authority by stealing himself. When he went away, Randolph also reported, almost grudgingly, that Johnny was "otherwise" known by the name "John Harris."[5]

The advertisement reveals other details. Before he became the property of Edmund Randolph, Johnny had been the enslaved servant of Peyton Randolph. Randolph was a well-known, long-time resident of the town of Williamsburg. Like most gentlemen of his day, he enjoyed many of the privileges of being born into one of the most prominent families in the colony. He was educated by private tutors. Sometime around 1739, he attended the College of William and Mary where he studied law. Later, he continued his education at Middle Temple in London. In 1744, he passed the bar. Four years after becoming a licensed attorney, Randolph

followed in the footsteps of his father. He likely earned the respect of his family, his contemporaries, and his colleagues when he was appointed attorney general of the colony of Virginia. That same year, he also became a member of the colony's House of Burgesses. In 1766, he was elected Speaker of the House.[6]

During the early years of the American Revolution, the elder Randolph served on the Committee of Correspondence. Later, when the colony's local leaders organized themselves into conventions after Lord Dunmore dissolved the House of Burgesses, and began meeting in private at the local Raleigh Tavern, Randolph was elected president. When the colony's leaders considered a split with Great Britain, he played a prominent role in those proceedings too. Before his death in 1775, he served as the presiding officer of the first, second, and third Continental Congresses.[7]

Like many of his contemporaries in Virginia, Peyton Randolph was a grandee whose life was inextricably connected to slavery. He enslaved twenty-seven people. Among the many members of his fictive family: a mulatto man he named Johnny or, as the Black Virginian preferred to call himself, John Harris. Like many of his contemporaries, Randolph thought himself a patriarch. Like William Byrd II, who took pride in his fatherly role, the resident of Williamsburg might have shared the attitude of the Westover grandee who boasted to an English aristocrat in 1726: "I have a large Family. . . . Like one of the Patriarchs, I have my Flocks and my Herds, my Bond-men and Bond-women, and every Soart of Trade amongst my own Servants, so that I live in a kind of Independence on every one but Providence. . . . I must take care to keep all my people to their duty."[8]

John Wollaston's portrait of the distinguished Virginia dignitary certainly captures this high regard in which he held himself. Like most of his colleagues, the robust Speaker is a self-styled gentleman of refinement and taste. In the oil painting, the Speaker is shown wearing a gray wig. The color of his headpiece signified at once time and wisdom. It also embodied the politics of deference in which a selected few could and did demand respect and acquiescence from others. Another sign of his status, the brown jacket and waistcoat that Randolph sports had likely been imported from Great Britain. A hat is shown tucked under his left arm as he gestures with his right hand. His frame is portly, if not stout, betraying a life of many comforts. Thomas Jefferson apprehended these sentiments best when he observed of his cousin: "[A]ltho' not eloquent, his matter was so substantial that no man commanded more attention; which, joined with a sense of his great worth, gave him a weight in the House of Burgesses which few ever attained." More explicitly put, Randolph thought himself not only a patriarch, but also a gentleman.[9]

In Randolph's household, Johnny had been one of several domestics. He was possibly the most trusted member of Randolph's enslaved family. For, as his nephew tells it, the mulatto man "waited upon my uncle." According to Julie Richter's study of the enslaved members of Randolph's household, the younger Randolph's passing reference concealed

Peyton Randolph, John Wollaston, mid-18th century, oil on canvas. VMHC

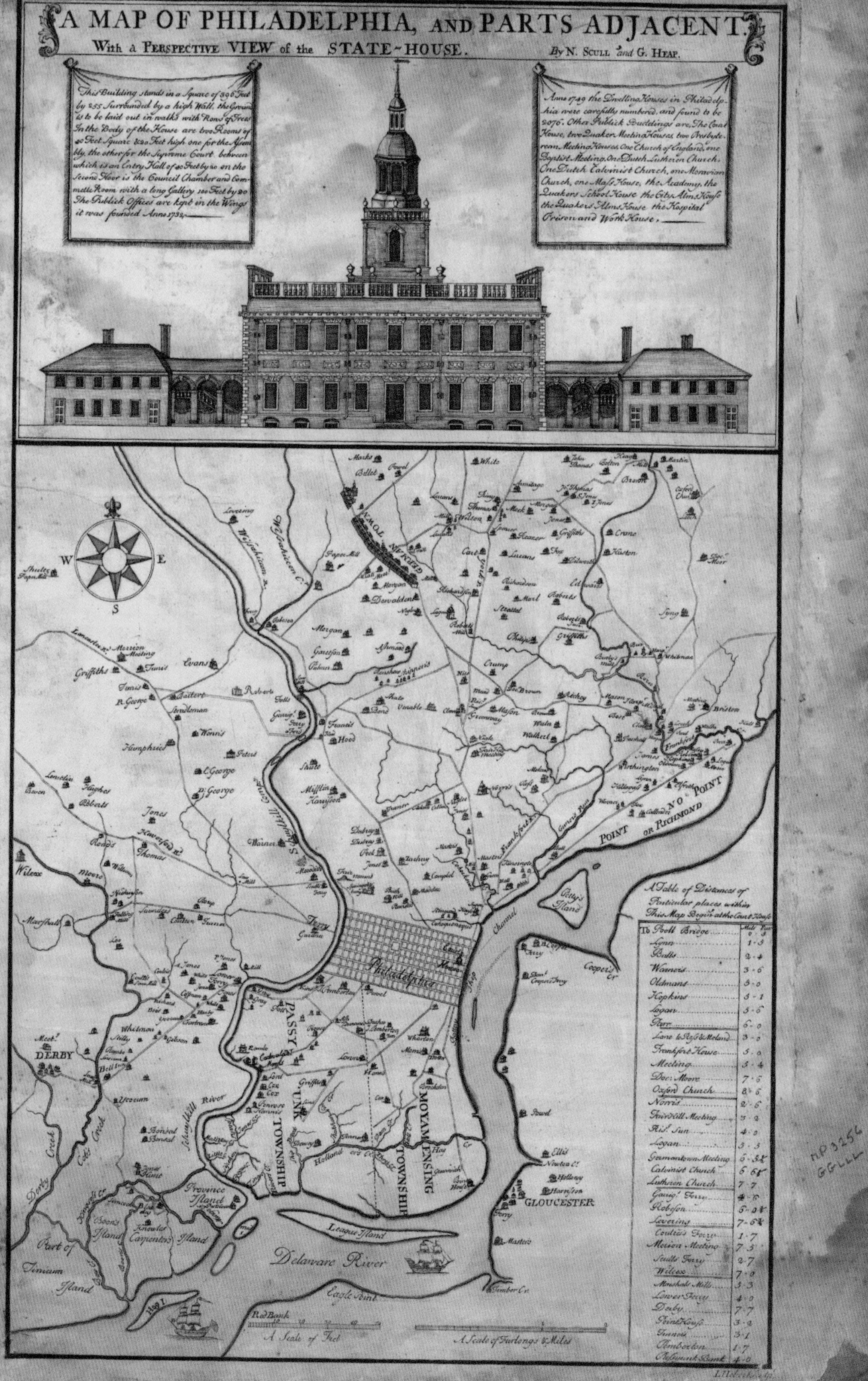

A MAP OF PHILADELPHIA, AND PARTS ADJACENT.
With a PERSPECTIVE VIEW of the STATE-HOUSE.
By N. SCULL and G. HEAP.
This Building stands in a Square of 396 Feet by 255 Surrounded by a high Wall, the Ground is to be laid out in walks with Rows of Trees In the Body of the House are two Rooms of 40 Feet Square & 20 Feet high one for the Assembly, the other for the Supreme Court between which is an Entry Hall of 40 Feet by 20 on the Second Floor is the Council Chamber and Committee Room with a long Gallery 100 Feet by 20 The Publick Offices are kept in the Wings it was founded Anno 1732.
Anno 1749 the Dwelling Houses in Philadelphia were carefully numbered, and found to be 2076. Other Publick Buildings are, The Court House, two Quaker Meeting Houses, two Presbyterian Meeting Houses, One Church of England, one Baptist Meeting, One Dutch Lutheran Church, One Dutch Calvinist Church, one Moravian Church, one Mass House, the Academy, the Quakers School House the City Alms House the Quakers Alms House the Hospital Prison and Work House.
W
E
S
GERMAN TOWN
Philadelphia
PASSY UNK TOWNSHIP
MOYAMENSING TOWNSHIP
DERBY
GLOUCESTER
POINT NO POINT OR RICHMOND
Schuylkill River
Delaware River
League Island
Province Island
Carpenters Island
Tinicum Island
Red Bank
A Scale of Feet
A Scale of Furlongs & Miles
A Table of Distances of Particular places within This Map Begin at the Court House
To Pooll Bridge 0 3
Lynn 1 3
Butts 2 4
Warners 3 6
Oldmans 3 0
Hopkins 3 1
Logan 5 6
Parr 6 0
Lane to Rx & Moland 3 0
Frankfort House 5 0
Meeting 3 4
Doc: Moore 7 6
Oxford Church 8 6
Norris 2 6
Fairhill Meeting 3 2
Risg Sun 4 0
Logan 3 3
Germantown Meeting 5 5½
Calvinist Church 6 6½
Lutheron Church 7 7
Gaug: Ferry 4 6
Robeson 6 0½
Levering 7 6½
Coulter's Ferry 1 7
Merion Meeting 7 3
Sculls Ferry 2 7
Wilcox 7 0
Marshals Mills 3 3
Lower Ferry 4 0
Darby 7 7
Point House 3 2
Tinnons 3 1
Pemberton 1 7
Passyunk Point 4 0

more than it revealed. By her account, the mulatto bondservant occupied a much more prominent place in his enslaver's life. He was described as the "Speaker's Man." In addition to serving Randolph as a waiter, he had been his personal body servant. In the mornings, he helped Randolph prepare. After styling his wig, he helped him dress. When not tending to Randolph's appearance, Johnny ran errands on behalf of the Williamsburg gentleman. On a few occasions, extant records demonstrate, the enslaved man even received tips from others while he worked in his enslaver's stead. Like other personal enslaved servants, Johnny wore the livery of Randolph, a sign of the close bond between the two.[10]

Almost obscured within Edmund Randolph's passing reference to the enslaved man's occupation is one aspect of the ideological origins of the American Revolution within enslaved communities. Simply put, like many of his Black contemporaries, Johnny learned about the American Revolution by word of mouth. Almost buried in the younger Randolph's description of the former Speaker's Man is the uncelebrated story of how many Black Virginians in the Chesapeake learned of the developing crisis between Great Britain and her North American subjects. To be sure, like most, if not all, personal servants, the Speaker's Man was privy to the revolutionary talk of the day. Because he had been Peyton Randolph's valet, he witnessed firsthand the transformation of the American rebellion into something more. Before the news of the American Revolution was type set in the printing presses of the day, Johnny, and likewise other enslaved body servants, were made aware of what was occurring in Virginia and in other colonies. In the near oblique spaces in Randolph's parlor, dining hall, and other chambers of the family abode, the Black Virginian listened as the Speaker and his contemporaries discussed their grievances about their British counterparts. When Thomas Jefferson's *Summary View of the Rights of British America*, for example, was read aloud, Johnny was there. "I distinctly recollect," the younger Randolph wrote in his history of Revolutionary Virginia, "the applause bestowed on" the resolutions "when they were read to a large company at the house of Peyton Randolph, to whom they were addressed."[11]

He also considered, albeit in private, the arguments between Patrick Henry and Peyton Randolph as the two leading Virginians debated over the future of the colony. Purportedly, when the former declared, "Give me liberty or give me death," Randolph's valet was there, if not nearby, as Hanover County's favorite son called his contemporaries to action. According to Julie Richter's study, the 'Speaker's Man' accompanied Randolph to meetings of the House of Burgesses. He received letters and other communiqués from important leaders in other colonies. When Randolph traveled to Philadelphia to meetings of the Continental Congress, Johnny went with him. When the Continental Association charged the "British Ministry" for the "unhappy Situation" in which the Parliament persisted in its efforts "for enslaving these Colonies," the Speaker's Man was adjacent to hear those words read aloud. Likewise, when the Congress debated the matter of the slave

A Map of Philadelphia and Parts Adjacent, Nicholas Scull and George Heap, 1752. Library of Congress

trade and moved to abolish the colonies' relationship with the infamous business of importing African people, the enslaved man was either in attendance, that is accompanying Randolph, or, at the very least, within hearing distance. The enslaved body servant learned of the Revolution in other ways as well. During his time in Philadelphia, for example, the mulatto was permitted the privilege of running an errand for Thomas Jefferson who tipped him seven shillings and six pence for his services. While he worked for the first apostle of America's democracy, Johnny likely learned more about the impending crisis. Within these varied settings, be it in Virginia or in Philadelphia, it is difficult to imagine the enslaved man not being *present* as the news of the crisis was debated and as news of those debates began to spread.[12]

In either case, in this manner, most enslaved people in Virginia, and likewise elsewhere, learned about the American Revolution. As household servants like Johnny tended to their enslaver's needs, they became aware of the political discourses of the day. Rendered invisible, like the protagonist in Ralph Ellison's first novel, they not only learned about the Revolution, but also shared what they learned with one another. Away from the watchful eyes of their enslavers, they discussed the burgeoning crisis among themselves. They considered the gravity of the historic moment in which they lived. In hidden places, beyond the margins of their enslaver's lives, Johnny and other members of the enslaved community began planning their response to the American Revolution.[13]

By 1777, the Speaker's Man had joined the ranks of those Black revolutionaries. Not long after he had been bequeathed to Peyton Randolph's nephew, the mulatto bondservant, whom his former enslaver valued at £100 in his 1776 probate inventory, declared his own independence and left Edmund Randolph's place in Williamsburg. Ironically, when he stole away, he stole not only himself, but also the clothing he had been issued. Judging from the description documented in the advertisement printed in the *Virginia Gazette* for the fugitive's apprehension, most of the articles of the clothing he carried away were imported from Great Britain. The elder Randolph, like many of his contemporaries, continued to import British wares despite the politics of the day. Well into the Revolutionary era, as Linda Baumgarten's study of clothing in early America shows, several members of the well-to-do patriots did not always practice what they themselves preached to others. That more than likely explains why instead of politicized homespun articles of clothing, John Harris "took with him . . . a green broadcloth coat, and a new crimson waistcoat and breeches, a light coloured Bath coating great coat, a London brown Bath coating close bodied coat, a pair of old crimson cloth breeches," as well as "some [additional] changes of clothes."[14]

There is no known portrait of Johnny and Peyton Randolph that shows the two together, but other examples of colonial portraiture do exist that capture the familial bonds that existed between masters and their personal slaves. In John Trumbull's 1780 portrait of George Washington, for example,

George Washington and William Lee, John Trumbull, 1780, oil on canvas. The Metropolitan Museum of Art, Bequest of Charles Allen Munn, 1924

the artist documents the complex relationship between the general and his personal bondservant, Billy Lee. Not surprisingly, Washington occupies the center of the portrait. In the margins of the canvas, however, Trumbull included the image of His Excellency's most trusted slave. Although Washington is depicted as a towering figure, standing on a bluff above the Hudson River, Billy Lee is shown on horseback, ready to answer his master's every beck and call. He waits patiently, wearing a scarlet turban. Like Johnny, Billy Lee's proximity to Washington afforded him, albeit unintentionally, access to information that could prove dangerous in the hands of the enslaved.[15]

Rhys Isaac and Sandra Gustafson's studies of colonial America further highlight the vital role orality played in Johnny's Virginia. Before 1800, information conveyed by word of mouth informed and determined public opinion. Like many early Americans who were inspired by the passionately expressed ideas of the Revolution, the Speaker's Man, as well as other Black Virginians, left after witnessing their enslavers and other whites in the colony publicly denounce their king in his less than compassionate attempts to govern their behavior. Throughout the burgeoning crisis in British America, Gustafson noted, the words of the American Revolution were not simply read aloud, as had been the custom; they were performed. From Massachusetts to Georgia, the news of the colonists' troubled relationship with England spread orally. Moreover, central to those public independence declarations is how the Great Awakening shaped how words were conveyed. The evangelical movement not only transformed profoundly the way in which early Americans related and communicated with one another, but it also fired the imaginations of the people who increasingly came to see themselves as "Slaves" to the king of Great Britain. Likely to the dismay of those persons who were held captive, early Americans reimagined the bonds that tied them with England.[16]

In Revolutionary Virginia, the oratorical genius of Patrick Henry captures best the ways in which the colony's literary and oral culture merged with the fiery evangelical sentiments of the day and inspired Virginians from all walks of life. Combining what appeared to many of his contemporaries as a frenzied blend of shifting vocal pitches and tones, punctuated by a variety of gestures and facial expressions, the Virginia statesman mastered the intertwined arts of rhetoric and moralizing persuasion. Imitating the oratory style of Samuel Davies and other Great Awakening ministers, Henry performed the word. His animated presentations of words that he either memorized or inscribed on paper or had set in print found a receptive audience throughout his native Virginia. Thomas Jefferson, for example, thought Henry "the greatest orator that ever lived."[17]

Henry's genius, however, could not be confined to just his colleagues or to other white Virginians not of his station. Quite the contrary; as both Rhys Isaac and Sandra Gustafson's studies show, Henry's dramatic musings were available to everyone who had ears. That included free and enslaved Virginians. Randolph's Johnny likely had a front seat, adjacent to that of

Patrick Henry, Thomas Sully, 1851, oil on canvas. VMHC, Gift of Thomas Sully

his enslaver, to hear Patrick Henry speak. On several occasions, after he had retired for the evening to the Randolphs' domicile, he likely shared with the other enslaved members of the Speaker's fictive family what he had witnessed firsthand. The Speaker's Man might have even reenacted aspects of Henry's lively performances. Among those Black Randolphs who likely enjoyed the valet's retelling of events was Eve, the personal enslaved servant to the Speaker's wife, who would later run away with her son George not long after Peyton Randolph's death in 1775. In this manner, the contagion of the American Revolution not only got out, but also found an audience among Black Virginians who were already caught up in the throes of their own unique revolution.[18]

When not contemplating the speeches of their white counterparts, Black people in Virginia learned about the conflict by following the news for themselves in manuscript form, if not in print. Although most learned of the Revolution by eavesdropping, some enslaved Virginians followed the events by secretly reading about them on public bulletins posted in communal places. As their enslavers and other white Virginians passionately recast their familial bonds with Great Britain, that is as they took off the shackles and chains of their mother country, members of their enslaved families listened in. If not by news items affixed to the wall or the doors that were used to communicate the political discourses of the day, literate Black people learned of the struggle for independence when they happened across letters or printed documents in their enslavers' homes that pertained to current affairs. That had certainly been the case with Johnny, who acted as Peyton Randolph's aide and who routinely related letters and private communiqués between the Speaker and his peers.

In addition to disclosing that fact, Edmund Randolph's ephemeral observation regarding Johnny's education reveals yet another avenue through which enslaved communities in Virginia and elsewhere learned of the crisis between Great Britain and her North American subjects. The gray-eyed man, the resident of Williamsburg explained, "can read and write tolerably well." In this reference, Randolph shows us another part of the ideological origins of the American Revolution among Virginians of African descent. In Johnny's endeavor to "pass for a freeman," Randolph seemed to suggest that the fugitive's education might have played some role in his declaration of independence. Unlike most enslaved Virginians, who were prohibited from learning to read and write, the mulatto man was able to follow the news of the rebellion while he served as Peyton Randolph's valet. That is, as he waited on his master inside and outside public places, like the Raleigh Tavern that served as the ad hoc meeting house for the disbanded House of Burgesses, the Speaker's Man could not help but to follow easily news of current events which was discussed in private, or that was published, if not posted on the many community bulletins that peppered Williamsburg.[19]

The younger Randolph's reference to Johnny's education begs the question: how did Johnny learn? In an era in which enslavers

Patrick Henry Arguing the Parson's Cause at Hanover Courthouse, George Cooke, about 1830, oil on canvas. VMHC

did not think it either wise or necessary to instruct the fictive members of their families, because such knowledge could prove the ruin of their property, how did the mulatto man learn to read? Moreover, how did he learn to write?

Records suggest several possibilities. Johnny might have been taught, for example, by Peyton Randolph, who thought his education a necessary part of his duties. Given his prominent place in Randolph's household, the valet could have been taught by Peyton Randolph himself, if not a family tutor. Despite the threat that slave literacy posed to the authority of the gentry class in Virginia, some enslavers educated members of their enslaved families because such lessons proved not only beneficial to their needs, but also a real manifestation of their Christian faith. In observance of the Apostle Timothy's injunction, to "give attendance to reading, to exhortation," they instructed their slaves. Whether for religious or personal reasons, both Johnny and the elder Randolph benefited from the former's education. For as Peyton Randolph's valet, he likely assisted his master in a variety of ways, working as his *amanuensis* who took notes and handled his correspondences.[20]

If not taught by Peyton Randolph himself, it is equally plausible that the Williamsburg grandee sent his man to Bruton Parish Church where he learned under the tutelage of the local parson, either William Yates or James Horrocks. As early as the 1720s, throughout the colony of Virginia, as well as in other parts of the British Empire, local leaders of the Anglican Church assumed, as part of their responsibility, the education of country-born Black people. The extant correspondence between the Bishop of London and his North American clergymen highlights this charge. In 1724, when asked by the bishop to describe the nature of Christian instruction, more than one-half of the church rectors in the Virginia colony responded. Most indicated work being done with the Black members of their congregations, which included literacy instruction. "I encourage the baptizing and catechizing of such of them as understand English," James Blair of the Bruton Parish in Williamsburg informed the bishop, "and exhort their Masters to bring them to Church." Blair's successors followed in his footsteps. So too did their contemporaries in other counties in the colony.[21]

There is also the possibility that Johnny might have taught himself to read and write. Unassisted by his enslaver, a tutor, or the local parson, the mulatto man learned by studying closely the actions of those around him. Like William Grimes, a Virginia runaway who escaped enslavement in 1814, the mulatto man acquired a knowledge of letters by means of his own design. Consequently, while Grimes would later write perhaps the earliest known slave autobiography, Johnny's flight inscribed in print a slave narrative that predates that of the Black barber.[22]

The most likely explanation as to how the enslaved man learned to read and write is that he learned at the Williamsburg Bray School for free and enslaved Black children. Between 1724 and 1777, the Associates of Dr. Thomas Bray made it their mission to proselytize the Christian faith throughout the British Empire through biblical education. As slavery transformed England into a global power, well-to-do Britons and their counterparts in his majesty's colonies sought to reconcile their sense of piety with their newfound place in what appeared to have been an increasingly shrinking world. In their minds, with wealth came responsibility; the responsibility of ensuring the spiritual well-being of those persons whom they

Old Bruton Church, Williamsburg, Virginia, in the Time of Lord Dunmore, Alfred Wordsworth Thompson, 1893, oil on canvas. The Metropolitan Museum of Art, Gift of Mrs. A. Wordsworth Thompson, 1899

considered members of their extended fictive families and communities. An offshoot of the Society for the Promotion of Christian Knowledge (SPCK) and the Society for the Propagation of the Gospels in Foreign Parts (SPG), the Associates of Dr. Thomas Bray advocated biblical literacy to the enslaved in the New World.[23]

In Virginia, they collaborated with empathetic grandees who shared their beliefs that with wealth came certain responsibilities. Devout Anglicans, the Virginia members of the Associates assumed it was part of their duty as masters to educate the members of their enslaved families, even though their education was thought not only dangerous, but also a usurpation of the plantocracy that existed in the colony. In addition to imagining themselves as the modern-day sons of Abraham, they took on the patriarchal obligation of caring for their charges in both secular and non-secular matters. In many of their minds, religion engendered not only a sense of piety, but also hard work. Obedience represented a form of grace

View of the front of the Bray School, 1920–21, photograph. Special Collections, John D. Rockefeller, Jr. Library, The Colonial Williamsburg Foundation

through which one could potentially receive the reward of paradise in the afterlife. Among those Virginians who accepted the Associates' plan was Peyton Randolph.[24]

Between 1760 and 1774, the Associates operated a Bray school in the town of Williamsburg that taught free and enslaved people. By November 17, 1774, when the school closed its doors, a number of enslaved Virginians had learned "the true Spelling of Words," how to pronounce "& read distinctly." Recent archeological artifacts unearthed at one of the sites used for the school reveal evidence of the enslaved writing and practicing penmanship. In the school's fourteen-year history as many as 400 scholars, if not more considering the school's injunction that its students practice their lessons at home, received biblical instruction through letters.

Extant school records suggest that the Speaker's Man likely attended the school. Between 1762 and 1774, Peyton Randolph enrolled several of his enslaved children in the school. Two years after the school opened, he sent Aggy, a seven-year-old girl. After Aggy, the Speaker entrusted other members of his fictive family to the care of the school's mistress, Anne Wager. In 1765, he enrolled two of his enslaved boys: Roger and Sam. In 1769, another one of his boys by the name of Sam attended the school. Considering Johnny's important occupation, it is highly likely that Randolph enrolled the mulatto man at the school.[25]

The likelihood of the valet being educated at the Williamsburg school increases if we take into account the number of children Randolph had baptized at Bruton Parish. Of the twenty-seven people the Speaker enslaved at the time of his death, most were noted as members of the Anglican Church, and as such candidates to be educated at the Williamsburg Bray School. Fifteen of them—Effy, Charly, Lucy, Mars, Robin, Robert, Dimbo, Aggy, Coy, Sukey, Dabney, George, Lewis, Henry, and Charles—were children when they received the rite of passage. As the church register establishes, 28 percent or almost a full third of the infants who belonged to the colonial grandee also noted the names of their mothers, which demonstrated not only familial ties but also the complex nature of relationships between enslavers and their enslaved. Six others—James, Humphrey, Sarah, Jane, William, and Robert—were adults when they received the sacrament. Although Johnny's name does not appear in these extant records, it is nonetheless reasonable to assume that Peyton Randolph had his most important slave educated.[26]

Moreover, the Williamsburg Bray School was not the only school for free and enslaved Virginians operating in the colony. Officially, the Associates ran another Bray school in Spotsylvania County in Fredericksburg, Virginia. Between 1765 and 1772, the Fredericksburg Bray School taught as many as 100 free and enslaved people how to read and write. Unofficially, the Associates of Thomas Bray supported several parish schools that parsons had been operating in their glebes. In Hanover, Caroline, and Norfolk counties, Anglican ministers received parcels of books and instructional manuals from the Associates, along with the charge that they instruct Black people. Literacy rates documented in runaway slave advertisements not only underscore the success of these official and unofficial Bray schools, but also the way in which Johnny and other Black Virginians became aware of the American Revolution.[27]

Before Cornwallis's surrender at Yorktown in 1781, before Thomas Jefferson estimated that 30,000 enslaved people in the colony had fled, Johnny had become one of many Black Virginians who left his master during the turmoil brought by the American Revolution. Like most Black people, he learned by word of mouth. Like most of his contemporaries, the ideological origins of his American Revolution began in the shadows of his former enslaver's life. His awareness of the burgeoning crisis was reinforced by the letters, resolutions, and other news items that came across the Speaker's desk. As the Speaker's Man, Johnny was undoubtedly an important figure within the Black community in Williamsburg and, as news traveled

Edmund Randolph, unknown artist, about 1858, oil on canvas. VMHC

fast by word of mouth, in other Black communities elsewhere.[28]

All of that would change in 1775 with the death of his enslaver. While serving as the president of the third Continental Congress in Philadelphia, Peyton Randolph died while having dinner with his cousin: Thomas Jefferson. Not long after Randolph's death, the executors of his estate informed Johnny that he had been apprized at £100, and that he had been bequeathed to Edmund Randolph, the Speaker's nephew. Though extant records do not tell us much about the relationship between these two men, one thing seems apparent. Johnny thought he had been demoted. His loyalty to Peyton Randolph had gone unacknowledged. The Speaker's declaration of independence did not apply to him. No longer occupying a high place within his previous enslaver's life, he did not care much for his new one: the younger Randolph. As the tension between Great Britain and the power brokers in the Virginia colony intensified, the mulatto took to drinking, perhaps to excess or, as his new owner described the matter, the fugitive "is much addicted." Did he drink to excess before Peyton Randolph died? Had he been a drunkard when he was the Speaker's Man? Surviving records proffer an answer: no. Because such behavior would have reflected badly on his enslaver, compromising therefore the favored station he enjoyed in the household of the elder Randolph.[29]

Removed from his previous house, and relocated to Edmund Randolph's residence in Williamsburg, Johnny might have found solace in strong drink. Perhaps his drunkenness reflected the possibility that the Speaker's Man was mourning the death of the Speaker. For several years, the two men were inseparable. They dressed the same. They walked similarly. They enjoyed many of the same things. They might have even enjoyed them together.[30]

Whatever the case might have been, Johnny left shortly after the death of his enslaver. A few months after Peyton Randolph died, the supposed alcoholic gathered his clothing and a few other articles that he thought belonged to him and that he thought he would need, and he carried himself away. The story he left behind is an interesting one. During his time as the Speaker's Man, he did not elect to steal away. Nor did he appear remotely interested in the precarious endeavor of owning himself. Instead, for several years, he stayed put. Even though he did not own himself, he seems to have enjoyed his life as the Speaker's Man. Likely, Johnny was the most important Black person in the city of Williamsburg.

However, after Peyton Randolph's death, everything seemed to change for Johnny. Not long after returning to Virginia with Peyton's widow, Elizabeth, who had joined her husband in Philadelphia, the former valet likely grieved the passing of the elder statesman. He also likely mourned the loss of his previous self. In his melancholy, he drank, perhaps more than he had before. He tried to drown his sorrows in a bottle. He watched as his previous life became a distant memory. And, when Dunmore issued his infamous proclamation in November 1775, he likely observed, cautiously one might add, as a few of his friends dared to steal themselves. By December, mid-winter, Johnny decided

Table 3
Estimated Literacy Rates in Colonial Virginia

Years	Enslaved Population [a]	Percentage Literate [b]	Number Literate
1720–1729	27,000	1	270
1730–1739	40,000	1	400
1740–1749	65,000	3	1,950
1750–1759	105,000	4	4,200
1760–1769	140,500	7	9,835
1770	180,500	6	10,830
1779–1780	224,000	6	13,440

Sources:

a. United States Bureau of the Census, *The Statistical History of the United States, from Colonial Times to the Present; Historical Statistics of the United States, Colonial Times to 1970* (New York: Basic Books, 1976), 1,168; Philip D. Morgan, *Slave Counterpoint: Black Culture in the Eighteenth-Century Chesapeake and Lowcountry* (Chapel Hill: University of North Carolina Press, 1998), 61, 221. This category does not include the free Black population, which likely had higher rates of literacy.

b. Windley, *Runaway Slave Advertisements*; Smith and Wojtowicz, *Blacks Who Stole Themselves*; Hodges and Brown, eds., *"Pretends to Be Free"*; Bly, ed., *Escaping Bondage*; *Readex*; *Eighteenth-Century American Newspapers*.

that the time had come. In the politically and religiously charged climate of the American Revolution, he became John Harris, a free man who freed himself.[31]

In the end, the picture of John Harris is not just the story of how one former enslaved Virginian learned about the American Revolution. Nor is it the story of how most Black people became aware of the politically charged times in which they lived. Not discounting the significance of either one of those stories, the picture of John Harris is also the tragic tale of how often history has made otherwise important historical actors invisible. For in the absence of writing or explicit documentation, the life story of John Harris and likewise other enslaved people has been rendered silent. Unfortunately, it has been almost erased from the pages of history itself. In his *Silencing the Past*, Michel-Rolph Trouillot, for example, explained how the production of history is not only a destruction of memory, as Pierre Nora and others have claimed, but also a formulation of power. For traditional historical archives and ways of knowing the past, he noted, are inherently reductionist in that they reduce the life experiences and the stories of those who did not leave behind written or printed documents to the inert, voiceless, or inarticulate. The "Rules," the Haitian anthropologist and historian further explained, "enforce constraints that belie the romantic image of the professional historian as an independent artist or isolated artisan." The production of the archive is largely a process that "involves a number of selective operations" that celebrate the contributions of one select group over the contributions of others. As a result, most historians follow "the acknowledge[d] rules of their time," which in most instances disregard those who did not write. In this setting, the story of how Harris and other Black people learned about America's fight for independence is considered not as important as the hopes and aspirations of their white counterparts who left behind printed or written accounts of their experiences. Simply put, their story did not transpire because the notes of its occurrence have escaped traditional ways of knowing, i.e., writing or some other accepted form of archival evidence. The ideological origins of their unique American Revolution were not recorded and therefore did not exist. Thus, lost in Thomas Jefferson's estimation about the "30,000 slaves" who joined the British is the explicit recorded account that explains why they sided with them.[32]

Similarly, in his *Idea of History*, R. G. Collingwood not only rejected the proposition that all that is history must be literary in nature, but also encouraged subsequent generations of historians to fill the gaps that lie in between time and space with logic, prudence, and historical imagination. For between the voids that fill the traditional historical narrative, there exist picturesque moments of lives lived. In much the same way that dashes etched on grave markers simply indicate the dates when a person's life began and when it came to an end, so archival history conceals more than it reveals. Historical imagination, Collingwood insisted, bridges "the gaps between what our authorities [i.e., our sources] tell us." In his view, it "gives the historical narrative or description its continuity. That the historian must use his imagination is a commonplace." Most historians, however, would disregard imagination (however practical and insightful) because it is not tethered directly to a particular primary document.[33]

In its explication of the life story of John Harris and of the story of other Black Virginians and how they likely learned of the Revolutionary War in Virginia, this chapter attempts to reconstruct that past, using what Thomas Paine would consider obvious methods or a matter of common sense. To be sure, that past has been almost completely buried deep in the recesses of the archives. Imaginatively, this chapter attempts to rescue from history the memory of those Black Virginians who participated in America's struggle for independence. Sifting through the fragments they left behind, it attempts to explore their ideological origins within the context of their own unique experience as enslaved people in America. Ultimately, America's fight had been their fight, perhaps more so than their white contemporaries—such is that other facet of the picture of John Harris.

Chapter 5

Virginia's Families in Revolution

Karin Wulf

Revolutions are often reported as wars of men and ideas, but they have broad cultural and social roots and implications. For most people, men and women alike, the most direct context for the Revolution was the family, where they made decisions about how to participate and when, and where they felt the full impact of war most profoundly. From the deaths of loved ones in battle, in flight or in service, or from the intense disease environment, to the privations and stresses of war including dislocation, economic crisis, and the myriad other uncertainties they faced, men, women, and children across Virginia calculated the benefits and felt the impacts of revolution right at home. Virginians understood—and felt, and saw, and reported about—the American Revolution as a family matter. And they saw their neighbors, their comrades, and their enemies experience it the same way. Virginia families especially experienced the war as a conflict over ideas about freedom. In Revolutionary Virginia, the contrasting choice between slavery and freedom hit as close to home as conflicts between patriots and loyalists—and often these were fully entwined. We can learn a lot about both the Revolution itself and the lives of Virginians in the Revolution by paying attention to what often mattered most.

But as important as the family was as a locus of revolutionary experience, the history of families is challenging for us to corral. Families were as numerous and diverse as Virginia itself, but some of the same factors affected them all. What happened during the American Revolution that caused families to disperse, to leave their homes or places of residence? What were some of the immediate and longer-term impacts of the Revolution for families? What things changed—or did not change at all, or very little—during the Revolution? How important were the political as opposed to military events of the Revolution for families? And how can we possibly see into the feelings and decisions that families made during this chaotic time?

The historical sources created during the eighteenth century and preserved for us to use in the twenty-first century rarely offer us a full picture of families, let alone families in wartime. That so many Virginians were enslaved in the Revolutionary period,

Bedford Basin near Halifax (detail), unknown artist, about 1835, watercolor on paper. Library and Archives Canada, Acc. no. 1938-220-1

and that traditional historical sources rarely reflect the experiences of Indigenous people, compounds the challenge, as does the loss of so many of Virginia's early records during the Civil War.

We can look at the economic and military losses for families because those changes were documented through war and other records. We can look at how little family law changed across the eighteenth century, and how that would profoundly shape Revolutionary-era experiences. We can look at how both political and religious ideas wrenched families and communities apart in the crucible of revolution. And we can look to some of the better documented extended families to see, almost sideways, both their experiences but also how others whose lives left us fewer historical materials to work with were also affected by the war for independence and its aftermath. Together these glimpses of what were pervasive issues and developments for families can give us a better understanding of what the Revolution meant at home.

The effects of the Revolution on families were both immediate and long term. The Revolution consolidated and scattered all kinds of Virginia families, economically, geographically, and politically. For Cherokee families on the colonies' western edges, entangled in conflicts with settlers for generations, the Revolution would bring an intensification of political and armed conflict. For other Indigenous families in Virginia, the choices laid out by the emerging war between the colonists and the British were not always obvious ones. What would make their families and communities safer, more secure, in both the short and long term? For enslaved Virginians, whether to take the offer of freedom offered by the British was an equally complex question. In November of 1775, the last royal governor of Virginia, Lord Dunmore, had proclaimed free "all *indented servants*, *Negroes*, or others (appertaining to rebels) . . . that are able and willing" to join the British forces in support of the Crown. This was more than Virginia Patriots would ever offer to enslaved people.

Then when military forces were moving through Virginia, or when their own loved ones were off at war or caught behind changing enemy lines, families had to keep close track of one another. When George Washington and other military leaders exchanged correspondence about tactics and strategy during the war, the safety of their families and other families was never far from their mind. In a long and urgent letter in the first year of the war about troop placement, spies, and British maneuvers, one of Washington's trusted colonels wrote speaking freely about the issues at hand, then asked for the general's "Pardon [for] the Freedom I have used." It was only, he wrote, that the stress of the situation made him less than circumspect. For "the Love of my Country, a Wife & 4 Children in the Enemys Hands, the Respect & Attachment I have to you—the Ruin & Poverty that must attend me & thousands of others will plead my Excuse for so much Freedom" in writing to his general this way. War's impact on families ran right down the line to the ways that anxiety was communicated among military men. Even Washington himself worked with Martha Washington to keep her

Lord Dunmore's Proclamation, November 7, 1775, broadside. Courtesy of the Library of Virginia

By His Excellency the Right Honorable JOHN Earl of DUNMORE, His MAJESTY'S Lieutenant and Governor General of the Colony and Dominion of VIRGINIA, and Vice Admiral of the same.

A PROCLAMATION.

AS I have ever entertained Hopes that an Accommodation might have taken Place between GREAT-BRITAIN and this Colony, without being compelled by my Duty to this most disagreeable but now absolutely necessary Step, rendered so by a Body of armed Men unlawfully assembled, firing on His MAJESTY'S Tenders, and the formation of an Army, and that Army now on their March to attack His MAJESTY'S Troops and destroy the well disposed Subjects of this Colony. To defeat such treasonable Purposes, and that all such Traitors, and their Abettors, may be brought to Justice, and that the Peace, and good Order of this Colony may be again restored, which the ordinary Course of the Civil Law is unable to effect; I have thought fit to issue this my Proclamation, hereby declaring, that until the aforesaid good Purposes can be obtained, I do in Virtue of the Power and Authority to ME given, by His MAJESTY, determine to execute Martial Law, and cause the same to be executed throughout this Colony: and to the end that Peace and good Order may the sooner be restored, I do require every Person capable of bearing Arms, to resort to His MAJESTY'S STANDARD, or be looked upon as Traitors to His MAJESTY'S Crown and Government, and thereby become liable to the Penalty the Law inflicts upon such Offences; such as forfeiture of Life, confiscation of Lands, &c. &c. And I do hereby further declare all indented Servants, Negroes, or others, (appertaining to Rebels,) free that are able and willing to bear Arms, they joining His MAJESTY'S Troops as soon as may be, for the more speedily reducing this Colony to a proper Sense of their Duty, to His MAJESTY'S Crown and Dignity. I do further order, and require, all His MAJESTY'S Leige Subjects, to retain their Quitrents, or any other Taxes due or that may become due, in their own Custody, till such Time as Peace may be again restored to this at present most unhappy Country, or demanded of them for their former salutary Purposes, by Officers properly authorised to receive the same.

GIVEN under my Hand on board the Ship WILLIAM, off NORFOLK, the 7th Day of NOVEMBER, in the SIXTEENTH Year of His MAJESTY'S Reign.

DUNMORE.

(GOD save the KING.)

from becoming a pawn of the British, and she moved from place to place within and out of Virginia throughout the war. He regularly worried, writing at one point to criticize the habit of armies to take such prisoners: "I can hardly think that Lord Dunmore can act so low, & unmanly a part, as to think of siezing Mrs Washington by way of revenge upon me," but that he and his men had been working to keep her "out of his reach."[1]

In other words, families had to be keenly aware of and strategize as best they could for their own safety and economic security even amid the war and their political commitments. This was not new to the Revolution, as wars had swept through the colonies repeatedly. And the Revolution occurred against the backdrop of long-standing patterns and structures of family life which persisted throughout the colonial period and into the early United States—and even longer.

Some of the first, obvious, and ongoing impacts of the Revolution for Virginians would have been economic. This hit all kinds of families. With the disruption of trade, the tobacco market was imperiled, along with the circulation of other crops and goods throughout the Atlantic. Estimates of the economic crisis brought on by the war suggest the colonial economy may have shrunk by as much as 30 percent. For the largely agricultural economy, mostly dependent on selling crops, this meant that most households would have felt the privations of war—whether because they could not sell those crops or other goods, or because they could not then buy what they needed or wanted. The colonial economy ran mostly on exporting staple crops and importing finished goods, with a healthy amount of trade among neighbors for smaller items they could grow or make. In Virginia, this meant households—including enslaved people—had long been making and trading homespun cloth, as well as buying more polished and fashionable imported cloth. In the years leading up to the Revolution, protesting imported goods became a political posture, and wearing homespun became a mark of opposition to British taxes. But in the years of Revolution homespun became more of a necessity, and its production more burdensome.[2]

Then, the loss of men wounded or killed in the war might be the most immediate and long-standing way that Virginia families confronted the Revolution. Virginians wounded in war were mostly not in Virginia—the battles of Great Bridge and Yorktown notwithstanding, most Virginians who fought in the Revolution were fighting away from home. But when they did perish, the effect of their loss on their families and communities was profound. Among the first of those more than 1,700 listed in the Library of Virginia database of military dead for the American Revolution was Minny, a Black man and a pilot who was killed in the spring of 1776 on the Rappahannock River. As a pilot, Minny was among a skilled group, and the scale of Virginia's enslaved Black communities made for extensive kin ties if not the ability to form and hold households. The Scottish doctor Hugh Mercer, who had settled in Fredericksburg and then served as a general in Washington's army, was killed at the Battle of Princeton in early 1777. Mercer

Frock coat, about 1780, cotton and wool. The Colonial Williamsburg Foundation, Museum Purchase

Coat, England or Europe, 1760–80, silk and velvet. The Colonial Williamsburg Foundation, Acquired by Bargain/Sale from Diane S. Taylor

The Death of General Mercer at the Battle of Princeton, January 3, 1777, John Trumbull, about 1789–1831, oil on canvas. Yale University Art Gallery, Trumbull Collection

had married a Virginian and his widow never remarried, dying in 1791. We could assume that both men left families, and we might also assume that both of their families, though with dramatically different resources available to manage the long war to come, would have had extended kin around them. Whether their homes are known to us or unknown, whether they died in combat or during other calamities, whether they were poor or rich, white or Black, none of these men would have lived—or died—without consequence for their communities and their families.

Like Minny, Virginians began dying in what would become the Revolutionary War at least as early as 1776, some as combatants in the militia, others serving in the Continental Army. They came from all over the Commonwealth, though some are listed as having an "undetermined" home. They died in battle, like Minny and Mercer, but mostly from disease and other more pedestrian causes that plagued civilians and military alike. Gregory Adams, a private who died at Valley Forge in February of 1778, was already listed as sick in the first muster roll for his detachment in 1778. William Campbell, originally of Augusta County, died at Yorktown in 1781—but of illness, possibly a heart attack, and a month before the great battle. A brigadier general in the militia when he died, Campbell was originally buried at an in-law's home near Richmond but in the early nineteenth century descendants took him back to his own home and family cemetery in southwest Virginia.[3]

The foundations of colonial Virginia law and society were ideas and structures of family that framed how they would experience the Revolution. Derived from British law and religious ideas, there was an expectation that white men of property, even minimal property, would be the titular and functional heads of their household. All others would be dependents within those households, including all women and children, as well as servants and, of course, enslaved persons.

For men and women both, the ways that family law, which changed little from the colonial period into the period of the Revolution and early United States, reflected those ideas about hierarchy had a major impact. For white men, it was presumed that they could and would control their families' and households' economic lives. For women, the laws of coverture and *partus sequitur ventrem* tightly—but with dramatically different impact on white and Black women—controlled their access to property and freedom. Coverture was the law that sharply restricted married women's ability to act as independent persons. It made any property that married women brought to their marriage either the property of their husband outright, or his to manage and profit from. The presumption was that the head of household would do so for the benefit of his family.

This presumption about men's role as head of household informed not only family life but also the ways that family life intersected with public, political life. Only white men of property could be voters or full political participants. But that property that enabled men's political lives could derive from their wives. As a bill in the Virginia legislature late in 1776 put it, "every free white man who at the time of elections for delegates or Senators . . . shall have been for one year preceeding in possession of twenty five acres of land with a house and plantation thereon or one hundred acres of Land without a house or plantation . . . in his own right or in right of his wife shall have a vote."[4]

Marriage was a privilege allowed only for free people, and because so few people of color could formally marry, coverture was a law that defined most free white women's experience of family life. If single or widowed, these women could own property—which meant they could buy and sell and even bequeath it when they died. In Virginia, though living in long-term widowhood was not as common as in colonies with major cities, like everywhere the war touched, the Revolution brought new contexts to married women's responsibilities. If their husbands were absent or injured or killed, they regularly took on more overt and public responsibilities managing the household economy. This included putting more women, not only widows, in direct management of enslaved people. White women were always significant actors in the slave economy in that they bought, sold, and inherited enslaved people, but the Revolution added new dimensions to their role as enslavers.

Partus sequitur ventrem, loosely Latin for "children follow the belly," was the law that enslaved the children of enslaved women. Unlike other aspects of family law, such as coverture, that were rooted in British legal custom and practice, the laws of slavery were new to the colonial context. And *partus* was the most important of the myriad laws that developed to maintain this violent system. By the time of the Revolution, 40 percent of Virginia's population was enslaved—the second largest percentage and the largest number of enslaved people in the British mainland North American colonies. Most enslaved Virginians were born into slavery, not captured and forcibly brought from Africa, but raised into a system of violent oppression for themselves and their families. The Revolution would force new contexts for enslaved women's and families' experiences, too.[5]

Some of the sharpest changes came with choices and conflicts that could expose families and households to more violence. When William Campbell died, his widow, Elizabeth Henry Campbell, became the executor of his estate. The war was concluding, but it had exposed intense conflicts in the backcountry where they had lived. Campbell had been a politician as well as a military man, and had become famous for leading Patriots both against the Cherokee and against Virginia Loyalists; he had been ruthless against both. Elizabeth now had to manage their estate, which included enslaved people. She would remarry another officer and Patriot-cum-politician, William Russell. Since she was the sister of the firebrand Patriot Patrick Henry, perhaps none of this was entirely new to her.[6]

The Campbells' backcountry community was roiled by war, and by the divided loyalties that made enemies of families and neighbors. In Virginia's upper valley, west of the Blue Ridge, including William Campbell's Washington County, Patriots and Loyalists battled ferociously. Campbell

Music and Dance in Beaufort County, attributed to John Rose, about 1785, watercolor on paper. The Colonial Williamsburg Foundation, Gift of Abby Aldrich Rockefeller

Elizabeth Henry Campbell Russell, unknown artist, n.d., oil on canvas. Courtesy of the South Carolina State Museum, Gift of Mr. Edmund R. Taylor, Ms. Eliza Taylor Shockley, & Ms. Mariana Taylor Manning

and his compatriots recruited soldiers and required them to sign "Articles of Association" which would serve to bind them and their families to the cause in the eyes of their community. Loyalists countered with their own oath-taking. The tension between the two groups, and accusations and suspicions within them, could make people feel like, as one Patriot put it, they could not trust anyone outside their family. The two groups threatened one another's families and property, including enslaved people. William Campbell was reputed to be vicious against Loyalists, and the Virginia legislature heard more than one complaint from families and neighbors about what were described as his unlawful actions, taking property, or administering the harshest justice without process. It was war.[7]

John Broady looked so much like Willliam Campbell that, in the heat of the Battle of King's Mountain in South Carolina, where men from Virginia's Upper Valley militias helped beat back the British efforts to energize southern Loyalists, people mistook him for the then-colonel. Campbell was described as tall and red-haired, like another Virginia Patriot leader, Thomas Jefferson. But Broady was not only represented as looking like Campbell but very explicitly described as a "mulatto." A mixed-race man, Broady was enslaved by the Campbells until 1793. The manumission of Broady was the work of Campbell's son-in-law Francis Preston, and reflected multiple layers of family context: "Whereas my negro man John (alias) John Broady, claims a promise of freedom from his master General William Campbell, for his faithful attendance on him at all times, and more particularly while he was in that army in the last war, and I who claim the said negro in the right of my wife, daughter of the said General William Campbell." Now recognized for his military service, Broady (or Broddy) had a son, Charles Joseph, born soon after gaining his freedom, and at least some of his descendants continued to live in Washington County.[8]

Slavery divided Virginia families in many ways. Enslaved families were wrenched or kept apart by enslavers; for enslaved Virginians, whether to run for freedom was always a consideration. During the Revolution, however, there were new costs and benefits to weigh as the British promised Black Virginians their freedom in exchange for their loyalty. Within six months of Dunmore's famous proclamation in 1775, offering freedom to those enslaved persons who would support the British, as many as a thousand Virginians escaped slavery to join his forces. Though Dunmore may have meant to extend his offer of liberation in exchange for loyalty to men who could fight, as many as half of those first thousand were women and children. In other words, families were on the move—together.[9]

Some Black loyalists indeed made it to British Canada after the Revolution and after the British made good on their promise of freedom—and, for many, this was another stop on their family migration. In 1783, Margaret Willus reported that she had gone to Nova Scotia "from Virginia four years ago" with her daughter Jenny, and that her baby daughter Judith "was born behind British lines." Judith Jackson ran for freedom in Norfolk pregnant and carrying a toddler, and

Bedford Basin near Halifax, unknown artist, about 1835, watercolor on paper. Library and Archives Canada, Acc. no. 1938-220-1

then joined Dunmore's troops as a laundress. She served for eight years in this capacity, which the authorities determined was enough to secure her and her children's freedom even after a claim was made for them to the British Board of Inquiry set up to resolve the claims of Loyalists to lost property including people they enslaved. Another Norfolk woman made a direct appeal to the Parliamentary commission for Loyalist claims. Chretia Weeks, a free Black woman, stated that "She, Her Husband and son Lived intirely on the produce of Their own Estate Till the Proclamation of Lord Dunmore was Declared, Signifying That the losses of all those who Joins the British Army Should be made good," that they fled with the British to New York and their home was burned. Her "Husband Ralph WEEKS was late Serjeant in the Black Company of Labourers" for nine years. For all these women, the Revolution had provided the possibility of greater freedom, and they seized it, alongside their families. Here was a change that revolution wrought.[10]

There are no firm figures, but estimates tell us that as many as 20,000 enslaved people chose to go to the British for the chance at freedom. We do not know exactly how many were from Virginia, but it seems safe to say that, given that Virginia had the largest total and the largest enslaved population of the colonies, it could have been half or more. We do know that enslaved Virginians left situations in cities like Norfolk, as well as both small and large plantations. They left enslavers who were obscure, and those who were prominent. Among those who left Thomas Jefferson's plantations were a woman called Black Sal and her three children, and Hannibal and Patty and their six children. The risks were serious, though it is hard to know if they would have been more endangered by staying or going—so many people died as smallpox and other diseases crashed through their communities and the British encampments and ships. Sal and her children all died; Hannibal and Patty died too, and only one of their children survived the war.[11]

Some family choices may seem more pragmatic to us from a distance of two and a half centuries, but others remain more abstract. How ideas about politics and religion intersected with the Revolution filled the printed pamphlets and other circulating texts of the period, and they tend to make plain how individual men may have committed themselves to action or allegiance. But they do not reveal how their families were part of those decisions or came to live with those choices. Religious beliefs were crucial to how many families thought about the potential for revolution. Virginia's official church was the Church of England, and it stressed loyalty to the king. The growing numbers of Baptists and Methodists, however, were already more restless with central authority. And although they were a small minority, for Virginia's Quakers, their pacifism was definitive. For all these groups, the intersection of revolution, religious commitments, and slavery was complex.

Among white Quakers, slavery had already been a cause of disagreement and disownment from their religion. For decades, and starting in earnest in the 1750s, Quakers were calling for consistency of their belief in spiritual equality, and for the manumission of all people enslaved by Quakers. For Quakers who lived in both the largest colony and the colony with the largest population of enslaved people this cut deeply, and many resisted. Virginia Quakers were a relatively small group and did not have the benefit of the large community of co-religionists as did those in the much larger Quaker communities of Philadelphia. The founder of Virginia's antislavery society, Robert Pleasants, had spent time in Philadelphia with kin among the Quakers there, and returned home to persuade his father and brothers to begin the process of manumitting more than 200 people they enslaved at their Henrico County plantation. In Virginia, however, only an act of the legislature could give people their freedom from slavery. But Pleasants and his family persisted. Just before and in the early years of the Revolution, they began crafting wills that would allow people to go free once the laws changed. This embrace of antislavery was a source of enormous conflict with other white Virginians.[12]

But there were other features of Quakerism that provoked controversy. Theologically, Quakers also professed to oppose violence in any form. Their pacifism—they called it neutrality—made them a target of derision and discrimination from Patriots across all the colonies. In the late summer of 1777, the Congress in Philadelphia resolved to inspect the political actions and sentiments of more than forty Quakers in the city and exiled over twenty of them to Virginia. Prompted by deep and long-standing suspicions about the Friends' pacifism, articulated most robustly and perhaps persuasively by John Adams, and by the discovery of a cache of documents from a Quaker meeting revealing Patriot movements and other sensitive information, Congress published its report and determination in the Philadelphia and other newspapers.

Within eight months the exiles were back. In the interim, Quakers throughout the newly independent states had rallied, pushing back not only against Adams's soft bigotry but also revealing the fraudulence of that packet of papers that had been the predicate for the exile. The families of the exiles and members of Winchester's Quaker community consistently raised questions about the treatment of conscientious objectors during times of war, and the specter of demonizing political differences. And for the next years of the Revolution and long after, the relationship of Quakers to the Revolution was fraught, and publicly so, as they negotiated and proclaimed vindication.

For the small Quaker community in Winchester, those eight months were a signal event. At the household level, it required management and rearrangement at best, producing dislocation, stress, and trauma. In Virginia, local officials struggled, and the local Quaker community struggled, to accommodate the exiles. In the longer term, the intersection of women's activism and advocacy for the exiles' release, including letters to George Washington and less overt tactics such as creating a supply chain to keep the men warm and fed over the winter, and the real and intensifying threats of beating back accusations of disloyalty—or treason—that prompted the

Quaker Meeting House, Winchester, Frances Benjamin Johnston, about 1930–39, photograph. Carnegie Survey of the Architecture of the South, Library of Congress, Prints and Photographs Division

exile in the first place, called back to Quaker martyrdoms of the seventeenth century. Families whose loyalties were in fact divided felt this rending as permanent. Some losses were indeed permanent. When the exiled men returned to Philadelphia in 1778, they left behind two of their number, buried in the cemetery of the Quaker meeting house in tiny Winchester, Virginia.

Although settler families could be divided by religion and politics, Indigenous families

John Mursh was Born may the 6. 1786
Robert Mursh was Born march the 24 1788
Sarah Mursh was Born march the 29.. 1790
Betsey Mursh was Born Novr the 14.. 1796
Rhoday Mursh was Born February the 21.. 1800
James Mursh the Son of John Mursh was Born Decr 21 1806

These are the Names of Robt Murshs Children & grand Children

Robert Mursh Pension Application, after 1806. National Archives and Records Administration, Washington, D.C.

could be caught in the conflicting currents and opportunities of the Revolution. Though most tribal communities in the west allied with the British, and most in the east allied with the Patriots, the same dynamics of dislocation and other stresses confronted them all. Examples of Indigenous men who served on both sides of the war reveal that their families would have felt the anxiety of having loved ones in the thick of the conflict's violence. The families of two men from Williamsburg, Robert Mursh and George Sampson, applied for veterans' benefits after the war in recognition of their service to the American cause. Sampson had died while with the army in New Jersey. Mursh and his wife had to submit their family histories as evidence of their need in the course of his application for a pension, describing his military service as a "Private" of the "Va Line," having first enlisted in 1776 in the "15th Regiment of the Virginia Continental Line" for three years, and then subsequently two other regiments. They shared a page from a family Bible record with their nine children and seven grandchildren, beginning with their daughter Kitty, born at the war's end in 1784.[13]

Some of the highest-profile American families split over the Revolution. Benjamin Franklin's son William had been, thanks in part to his famous father's networks, appointed the royal governor of New Jersey. Though he was expected to abandon his post once his father made plain his Patriot political allegiance, William Franklin remained steadfast in his support of the king, and later was an active and ardent Loyalist leader in New York until he finally left in 1782 for England. While in New York, he would have been part of the Loyalist networks that were facilitating Virginia's Black Loyalists. Back in Virginia, the Randolph family faced a split that was similarly dramatic to the Franklins'. John Randolph was appointed king's attorney in Virginia, and, as he watched the conflict with the colonies heat up, continued to advocate for and write about peaceful resolution. His brother Peyton Randolph, on the other hand, would be the Speaker at the first two independent Virginia Conventions, which John Randolph thought extralegal, and would go on to be President of the First Continental Congress. John Randolph left Virginia—for Scotland—with the fleeing Governor Dunmore. Though William Franklin never returned to America, John Randolph's remains came back to Virginia. His family had him buried in the chapel at William & Mary.

Other families rallied to support the Revolution or the Crown. But whether supporting or opposing the Revolution, or taking a more nuanced or calculated approach, families generally worked collectively. If men were to be away, women took on their labor and position at home in addition to their own. Family economics were always affected by the war, but also by the policies of the new state and national governments. And in the years after the Revolution, families would continue to be deeply affected by the choices they made, when they had choices, and the new world the Revolution ushered in. The losses they suffered during the war would reverberate through their experiences of the new American nation; though some families found themselves elated by the American victory, others felt more ambivalent.

As for Elizabeth Campbell Russell, her extended family wrestled with the challenges of freedom. At Patrick Henry's plantation, a family of three—Ralph, Miney, and their young daughter Molly Henry—left Virginia to join the British and to claim their freedom; they made it to New York and then to Nova Scotia. Meanwhile, Elizabeth and her second husband continued to live at the Campbell plantation, and then in 1795, a couple of years after he died, she manumitted several men and women, declaring that she felt they had "come into my possession by the direction of Providence, and conceiving from the clearest conviction of my conscience aided by the power of a good and just God, that it is both sinful and unjust, as they are by nature equally free with myself, to continue them in slavery." She had become a Methodist, and it was this religious conviction rather than her experience of the Revolution that would finally shape her approach to slavery, and to the people she had enslaved for so long. She would be a widow for the rest of her life, dying in the

1820s. A church in Saltville, Madam Russell Memorial United Methodist Church, still stands in her name.[14]

Rich or poor, Black, white, or Indigenous, Virginia's families had to navigate the cross-currents of revolution. Their ideas about politics were filtered through other experiences of slavery, or religion, or alliances of other kinds. And as mothers and fathers, wives and husbands, siblings, children, and extended kin, they had to make choices and decisions that reflected their own sense of what would best give themselves and their families the kind of liberty they sought.

Afterword

"The greatness of America lies not in being more enlightened than any other nation, but rather in her ability to repair her faults." – Alexis de Tocqueville, 1835

Our American experiment is unique in human history—a government of laws and not of individuals; a government *by the people* and *for the people*, founded on the self-evident truths that all are created equal and are endowed with the universal rights of *Life, Liberty, and the pursuit of Happiness*. In our first two and a half centuries, our nation, through the determination of its people, and with its unlimited capacity for reinvention and renewal, has progressed in its journey, working to fulfill by struggle and sacrifice the promise of our founding for all Americans.

The Semiquincentennial of the United States offers an opportunity—unique in our lifetime—to reflect more wholistically on our past, and to use the perspective gained to help us forge a brighter future. We must study and share our American and Virginian story—its fullness and complexity, its achievements and shortcomings—and honor the many voices that together forge one Commonwealth and one nation.

When done well, commemorations spark meaningful, lasting progress. They provide us with a timely reason to examine our past through an ever-wider lens—to tell better, richer, fuller history. Even more importantly, the commemoration of America's independence provides us with a timely call to recommit to our nation's founding ideals—*to repair our faults*—and to add to our collective story as we move ever closer to a *more Perfect Union*.

Give Me Liberty: Virginia & The Forging of a Nation, the marquee exhibition created through the partnership of the Virginia Museum of History & Culture and the Jamestown-Yorktown Foundation—two of Virginia's finest history organizations—is the product of just this sort of purposeful examination. Offering a compelling and fresh look at our past, this special exhibition embraces the sweeping history of America's founding and marks the origins of a revolutionary new nation. By recognizing and interpreting those Virginians, both well-known and unsung, for their role in shaping the new nation, *Give Me Liberty* inspires a deep appreciation for the local, continental and global forces that brought about a model of democratic government that would change the world.

Bringing together the scholarship of several preeminent subject matter experts and building upon the material included in the *Give Me Liberty* exhibition, this companion book allows us to dive even deeper in contextualizing this important historical period. It is intended to supplement the exhibition experience, prompt ongoing reflection, and connect the reader with this important national moment.

As Virginians and Americans engage with this national milestone, we hope the work of these two museums, the exhibition produced in partnership, and this companion book, can all add meaningfully to our individual and collective celebration, and to the path forward we all take together.

Jamie O. Bosket
President & CEO
Virginia Museum of History & Culture

George Washington and William Lee (detail), John Trumbull, 1780, oil on canvas. The Metropolitan Museum of Art, Bequest of Charles Allen Munn, 1924

SUPERIOR
RESERVED FOR THE IN
Q
Three
Michillimakinac
L. MICHIGAN
L. HURON
Montreal
1st Bat.
60.
15.
27.
Ofwegatchie
L. CHAMPLAIN
Crown p
Ticonder
L. GEORGE
Ft George
L. ONTARIO
Niagara
Ofwego
Ft Stanwix
No. 1
17. 60th 2. Bat.
Detroit
L. ERIE
Albany
NEW YORK
NEW
PENSYLVANIA
Elizabeth
New York
Amboy
Ft Pitt
42.
Philadelphia
18.
16.
46.
29.
26.
17.
MARYLAND
artres
OHIO R.
VIRGINIA
N. CAROLINA
Ft Prince George
No. 2.
Ft Charlotte
No. 3
S. CAROLINA
No. 4
Ft Augusta
Charles Town
No. 6.
GEORGIA
No. 7
Apalachie
Ft Frederica
No. 5
IDA
Penfacola
E. FL
ATLANTIC

Contributors

Antonio T. Bly is a professor of history at California State University, Sacramento. Before joining the history department at Sacramento State, he served as the Director of Africana Studies at Appalachian State University. He is a historian of early America and book history, and an active scholar and researcher. Dr. Bly's current research projects are a documentary history of fugitive Native Americans in eighteenth-century America and a study of freedom-seeking enslaved people in New England. He is the author of *Escaping Slavery: A Documentary History of Native American Runaways in British North America* (2022).

Woody Holton is a professor of history at the University of South Carolina. He teaches early American history, especially the American Revolution, with a focus on economic history and on Black Americans, Native Americans, and women. Dr. Holton is the award-winning author of several books, including *Forced Founders: Indians, Debtors, Slaves, and the Making of the American Revolution in Virginia* (1999); *Unruly Americans and the Origins of the Constitution* (2007); *Abigail Adams* (2009); and *Liberty is Sweet: The Hidden History of the American Revolution* (2021).

Sarah E. McCartney is assistant teaching professor at the National Institute of American History & Democracy and in the history department at the College of William & Mary. Her research focuses on the colonial Virginia backcountry (now present-day West Virginia) and the role of kinship, commerce, and the material culture of the Atlantic World in this frontier region's development. Dr. McCartney has published several articles and given presentations on the backcountry in the Revolutionary era.

Alan Taylor is the Thomas Jefferson Foundation Chair (Emeritus) at the University of Virginia. He is a scholar of the colonial, Revolutionary, and early Republic eras. Dr. Taylor is the author of numerous books, including *Liberty Men and Great Proprietors: The Revolutionary Settlement on the Maine Frontier, 1760–1820* (1990); *William Cooper's Town: Power and Persuasion on the Frontier of the Early American Republic* (1995), winner of the Bancroft Prize and the Pulitzer Prize; *The Divided Ground: Indians, Settlers, and the Northern Borderland of the American Revolution* (2006); *The Internal Enemy: Slavery and War in Virginia, 1772–1832* (2013), winner of the Pulitzer Prize; and *American Revolutions: A Continental History, 1750–1804* (2016).

Karin Wulf is a professor of history and the Beatrice and Julio Mario Santo Domingo Director and Librarian, John Carter Brown Library, at Brown University. She is a historian of gender, family, and politics in eighteenth-century British America. Before coming to Brown, Dr. Wulf was the Executive Director of the Omohundro Institute of Early American History and Culture, and a professor of history at William & Mary, and taught at American University and Old Dominion University. Her current book, *Lineage: Genealogy and the Power of Connection in Early America*, is forthcoming from Oxford University Press. She is the author and coauthor of numerous scholarly articles and several books, including *Milcah Martha Moore's Book: A Commonplace Book from Revolutionary America*, with Catherine La Courreye Blecki (1997); *Not All Wives: Women of Colonial Philadelphia* (2000); and *The Diary of Hannah Callender Sansom: Sense and Sensibility in the Age of the American Revolution*, with Susan E. Klepp (2010).

Cantonment of His Majesty's Forces in N. America according to the disposition now made & to be compleated as soon as practicable taken from the general distribution dated at New York 29th. March 1766 (detail), 1767. Library of Congress

Notes

Chapter 1

1. Resolutions and Association of the Virginia Convention of 1774 [August 1–6, 1774], *Founders Online*, National Archives, https://founders.archives.gov/documents/Jefferson/01-01-02-0091 (accessed July 15, 2024).
2. George Washington to John Posey, June 24, 1767, *Founders Online*, https://founders.archives.gov/documents/Washington/02-08-02-0001 (accessed July 16, 2024).
3. *The Annual Register, or A View of the History, Politicks, and Literature for the Year 1763* (London, Eng., 1764), 21; [Thomas Gage,] "Report of the Forts in North America . . . ," enclosed in Thomas Gage to Barrington, December 18, 1765, in Clarence Edwin Carter, ed., *The Correspondence of General Thomas Gage* (2 vols.; Hamden, Conn.: Archon Books, 1969), 2:319; John L. Bullion, "'The Ten Thousand in America': More Light on the Decision on the American Army, 1762–1763," *William and Mary Quarterly*, 3rd ser., 43 (1986): 646–57.
4. The Revenue (Sugar) Act: "all the monies [shall be] disposed of by parliament, towards defraying the necessary expences of defending, protecting, and securing, the British colonies and plantations in America." Great Britain, Parliament, "An act for granting certain duties in the British colonies and plantations in America [and] for applying the produce . . . of the duties to arise by virtue of the said act, towards defraying the expences of defending, protecting, and securing the said colonies and plantations. . ." [passed by the House of Commons, April 5, 1764] (*The Avalon Project*, Yale Law School, avalon.law.yale.edu/18th_century/sugar_act_1764.asp [accessed July 16, 2024]). The Stamp Act: "all the monies which shall arise by the several rates and duties hereby granted . . . shall be paid . . . towards further defraying the necessary expences of defending, protecting, and securing, the said colonies and plantations." Great Britain, Parliament, "An act for granting and applying certain stamp duties, and other duties, in the British colonies and plantations in America, towards further defraying the expences of defending, protecting, and securing the same," March 22, 1765 (*The Avalon Project*, avalon.law.yale.edu/18th_century/stamp_act_1765.asp [accessed July 16, 2024]).
5. William Byrd to John Perceval, July 12, 1736, in Marion Tinling, ed., *The Correspondence of the Three William Byrds of Westover, Virginia, 1684–1776* (2 vols.; Charlottesville: University Press of Virginia, 1977), 2:488; Christopher Leslie Brown, *Moral Capital: Foundations of British Abolitionism* (Chapel Hill: University of North Carolina Press, 2006).
6. Virginia House of Burgesses, Virginia Resolutions on Lord North's Conciliatory Proposal [June 10, 1775], *Founders Online*, https://founders.archives.gov/documents/Jefferson/01-01-02-0106 (accessed July 16, 2024).
7. Woody Holton, *Forced Founders: Indians, Debtors, Slaves, and the Making of the American Revolution in Virginia* (Chapel Hill: University of North Carolina Press, 1999), 62.
8. Ambrose Serle, journal, July 31/Aug. 1776, in Edward Howland Tatum, ed., *The American Journal of Ambrose Serle: Secretary to Lord Howe, 1776–1778* (San Marino, Calif.: The Huntington Library, 1940), 51–52; Isaac Samuel Harrell, *Loyalism in Virginia: Chapters in the Economic History of the Revolution* (Durham, N.C.: Duke University Press, 1926), 3–29; Emory G. Evans, "Planter Indebtedness and the Coming of the Revolution in Virginia," *William and Mary Quarterly*, 3rd ser., 19 (1962): 511–33.
9. *Report of the Record Commissioners of the City of Boston . . .* (39 vols.; Boston: Rockwell and Churchill, 1876–1909), 16:221–25; Nathaniel Ames, *An Astronomical Diary; or, Almanack for the Year of Our Lord Christ 1768: . . . Calculated for the Meridian of Boston, New-England, Latt. 42° 25' North* (New Haven, Conn.: Thomas and Samuel Green, 1768); Jill Lepore, *Book of Ages: The Life and Opinions of Jane Franklin* (New York: Alfred A. Knopf, 2013), 146.
10. George Washington to George Mason, April 5, 1769, *Founders Online*, https://founders.archives.gov/documents/Washington/02-08-02-0132 (accessed July 16, 2024).
11. Holton, *Forced Founders*, 95.
12. "The Association entered into by the American [Conti]nental Congress in Behalf of all the Colo[nies]," October 20, 1774, *Founders Online*, https://founders.archives.gov/documents/Jefferson/01-01-02-0094 (accessed July 16, 2024); South

Carolina Council of Safety to Stephen Drayton and William Ewen, January 1, 1776, in Philip M. Hamer et al., eds., *The Papers of Henry Laurens* (16 vols.; Columbia: University of South Carolina Press, 1968–2003), 10:604; Robert M. Weir, "South Carolina: Slavery and the Structure of the Union," in Michael Allen Gillespie and Michael Lienesch, eds., *Ratifying the Constitution* (Lawrence: University Press of Kansas, 1989), 206.

13. "The Association entered into by the American [Conti]nental Congress"; James Robison to Cuninghame and Company, March 31, 1775, in T. M. Devine, ed., *A Scottish Firm in Virginia, 1767–1777: W. Cuninghame and Co.* (Edinburgh, Scot.: C. Constable for the Scottish History Society, 1984), 20:177, 180; William Lee to Francis Lightfoot Lee, April 2, 1774, Arthur Lee Papers, Houghton Library, Harvard University; William Lee to Francis Lightfoot Lee, July 16, 1774, in Worthington Chauncey Ford, ed., *Letters of William Lee: Sheriff and Alderman of London: Commercial Agent of the Continental Congress in France: and Minister to the Courts of Vienna and Berlin, 1766–1783* (3 vols.; Brooklyn, N.Y.: Historical Printing Club, 1891), 1:86; Holton, *Forced Founders*, chap. 4.
14. Richard Champion, *Considerations on the Present Situation of Great Britain and the United States of America, With a View to Their Future Commercial Connexions. Containing Remarks upon the Pamphlet Published by Lord Sheffield, Entitled, "Observations on the Commerce of the American States;" and Also on the Act of Navigation* . . . (London, Eng.: John Stockdale, 1784), 269n, cited in Jacob M. Price, *Capital and Credit in British Overseas Trade: The View from the Chesapeake, 1700–1776* (Cambridge, Mass.: Harvard University Press, 1980), 8.
15. Mrs. Adams reported that General Gage had detailed a colonel and a lieutenant to look into the matter, but apparently nothing immediately came of it (Abigail Adams to John Adams, September 22, 1774, *Founders Online*, https://founders.archives.gov/documents/Adams/04-01-02-0107 [accessed July 16, 2024]; James Madison to William Bradford, November 26, 1774, *Founders Online*, https://founders.archives.gov/documents/Madison/01-01-02-0037 [accessed July 16, 2024]).
16. Benjamin Waller, deposition, in John Pendleton Kennedy, ed., *Journals of the House of Burgesses of Virginia, 1773–1776. Including the Records of the Committee of Correspondence* (Richmond, Va.: E. Waddey Co., 1905), 232; "Deposition of Dr. William Pasteur in Regard to the Removal of Powder from the Williamsburg Magazine," *Virginia Magazine of History and Biography* 13 (1905): 49; David John Mays, *Edmund Pendleton, 1721–1803: A Biography* (2 vols.; Cambridge, Mass.: Harvard University Press, 1952), 2:13–14.
17. *Virginia Gazette* (Purdie), September 8, 1775, 2–3; *Virginia Gazette* (Dixon and Hunter), September 9, 1775, 3; Holton, *Forced Founders*, 133–34; Tony Williams, *Hurricane of Independence: The Untold Story of the Deadly Storm at the Deciding Moment of the American Revolution* (Naperville, Ill.: Sourcebooks, Inc., 2008), 32–50; Andrew Lawler, *Fire and Sword: Revolutionary Virginia's Struggle for Freedom* (forthcoming).
18. *Virginia Gazette* (Purdie), October 27, 1775 (supplement); *Virginia Gazette* (Pinkney), November 2, 1775, 3; Holton, *Forced Founders*, 134; Lawler, *Fire and Sword*; "Lord Dunmore's Proclamation, 1775: A Spotlight on a Primary Source by John Murray[,] Lord Dunmore," The Gilder Lehrman Institute of American History, *History Resources*, gilderlehrman.org/history-resources/spotlight-primary-source/lord-dunmores-proclamation-1775 (accessed July 16, 2024). Though Dunmore might have taken the name for his all-Black regiment straight from the Bible (for instance from Psalms 68:31: "Ethiopia shall soon stretch out her hands unto God"), it is also possible that a Whig newspaper gave him the idea when it sarcastically called the pilot, Joseph Harris, Dunmore's "Ethiopian director" (*Virginia Gazette* [Dixon and Hunter], September 23, 1775, 3).
19. "Examination of a Deserter from Staten Island," August 14, 1776, in Peter Force, ed., *American Archives. Fifth Series. Containing a Documentary History of the United States of America, from the Declaration of Independence, July 4, 1776, to the Definitive Treaty of Peace with Great Britain, September 3, 1783* (3 vols.; Washington, D.C.: M. St. Clair Clarke and P. Force, 1848–53), 1:996.
20. Cassandra Pybus, *Epic Journeys of Freedom: Runaway Slaves of*

the American Revolution and Their Global Quest for Liberty (Boston: Beacon Press, 2006).

21. Archibald Cary to Richard Henry Lee, December 24, 1775, in Paul P. Hoffman and John L. Molyneaux, eds., *The Lee Family Papers, 1742–1795* (microfilm; Charlottesville, 1966), reel 2.
22. Edmund Burke, speech, February 6, 1778, in Edmund Burke, *The Speeches of the Right Honourable Edmund Burke in the House of Commons, and in Westminster-Hall* (4 vols.; London, Eng.: Longman, Hurst, Rees, Orme, and Brown, 1816), 1:399 (my thanks to Andrew Lawler for this reference); Thomas Paine, *Common Sense; Addressed to the Inhabitants of America . . .* (Philadelphia, 1776), 59; Archibald Cary to Richard Henry Lee, December 24, 1775.
23. Andrew Lawler, *A Perfect Frenzy: A Royal Governor, His Black Allies, and the Crisis That Spurred the American Revolution* (New York: Atlantic Monthly Press, 2025).
24. Francis Lightfoot Lee to Landon Carter, April 9, 1776, and May 21, 1776, in Paul Hubert Smith et al., eds., *Letters of Delegates to Congress, 1774–1789* (26 vols.; Washington, D.C.: Library of Congress, 1976–2000), 3:500–501 ("licentiousness" and "old Government" quotations), 4:57 ("internal peace" quotation); Edward Rutledge to Ralph Izard, December 8, 1775, in ibid., 2:462–63; Richard Henry Lee to Patrick Henry, April 20, 1776, and Richard Henry Lee to Robert Carter Nicholas, April 30, 1776, both in James Curtis Ballagh, ed., *The Letters of Richard Henry Lee* (2 vols.; New York: The Macmillan Company, 1911), 1:177, 184; John Page to Thomas Jefferson, April 26, 1776, *Founders Online*, https://founders.archives.gov/documents/Jefferson/01-01-02-0151 (accessed July 16, 2024).
25. Robert Wormeley Carter diary, April 1, 1776, Special Collections Research Center, Swem Library, College of William and Mary; Charles Lee to Patrick Henry, May 7, 1776, in Henry Edward Bunbury, ed., *The Lee Papers . . . 1754–1811*, Collections of the New-York Historical Society for the Year 1871–1874 (4 vols.; New York: Printed for the New-York Historical Society, 1872), 2:3; Landon Carter to George Washington, May 9, 1776, *Founders Online*, https://founders.archives.gov/documents/Washington/03-04-02-0195 (accessed July 18, 2024).
26. Resolutions of the Virginia Convention Calling for Independence, May 15, 1776, *Founders Online*, https://founders.archives.gov/documents/Jefferson/01-01-02-0152 (accessed July 18, 2024); George Mason, first draft of the Virginia declaration of rights [c. May 20–26, 1774], Virginia convention, final draft of the declaration of rights, June 12, 1776, in Robert A. Rutland, ed., *The Papers of George Mason, 1725–1792* (3 vols.; Chapel Hill: University of North Carolina Press, 1970), 1:277, 287; Eric Slauter, "Rights," in Edward G. Gray and Jane Kamensky, eds., *The Oxford Handbook of the American Revolution* (New York: Oxford University Press, 2013), 454–56.
27. Jefferson had used very similar language in denouncing the Navigation Acts a year earlier, but it is possible that, in the Declaration, he meant for this phrase also to refer to the laws Congress had passed in 1775 closing the few loopholes in Britain's monopoly of American trade as punishment for colonial protests (Virginia House of Burgesses, resolutions on Lord North's conciliatory proposal, June 10, 1775, Declaration of Independence [final draft], *Founders Online*, https://founders.archives.gov/documents/Jefferson/01-01-02-0106 [accessed July 18, 2024]).
28. Declaration of Independence.
29. Resolutions of the Virginia Convention Calling for Independence, May 14, 1776; George Washington to Artemas Ward, July 9, 1776, *Founders Online*, https://founders.archives.gov/documents/Washington/03-05-02-0184 (accessed July 18, 2024); Rhode Island assembly, July 1776, Maryland Convention, August 17, 1776, John Rutledge, speech to the South Carolina legislative council, September 19, 1776, in Force, ed., *American Archives*, 5:1:475, 993, 5:2:392.
30. Slauter, "Rights," 457–59.
31. See Franklin D. Roosevelt, speech at the dedication of the Jefferson Memorial, April 13, 1943, University of California, Santa Barbara, *The American Presidency Project*, https://www.presidency.ucsb.edu/documents/address-the-dedication-the-thomas-jefferson-memorial-washington-dc (accessed July 18, 2024).

Chapter 2

1. This essay draws from Woody Holton's scholarship, which is

foundational for any historical research on Virginia's backcountry region in the Revolutionary era. Although Holton focuses broadly on the maneuverings of the political elites, this essay focuses more narrowly on those who were impacted by those actions (see Holton, *Forced Founders: Indians, Debtors, Slaves, and the Making of the American Revolution in Virginia* [Chapel Hill: University of North Carolina Press, 1999]). Historical scholarship on Virginia's "near backcountry" region during the American Revolution is often overshadowed by attention to the Ohio Country and frontier regions of western Pennsylvania and the Great Lakes. Though set in a different geographic place, this essay draws from and interacts with themes in some of those works (see Patrick Griffin, *American Leviathan: Empire, Nation, and Revolutionary Frontier* [New York: Hill and Wang, 2007]; Patrick Spero, *Frontier Rebels: The Fight for Independence in the American West, 1765–1776* [New York: W. W. Norton & Company, 2018]).

2. *Virginia Gazette* (Dixon and Hunter), March 11, 1775, 3; *Virginia Gazette* (Pinkney), March 16, 1772, 3; *Virginia Gazette* (Purdie), March 24, 1775, 3.
3. "Freeholders" were adult white males over the age of twenty-one in the colony who had "an estate of freehold, or other greater estate" that comprised at least 100 acres of land (if no settlement be made upon it), or twenty-five acres with a house or plantation in the possession of him or his tenants, or property in a city or town (see William Waller Hening, ed., *Statutes at Large; Being a Collection of All the Laws of Virginia from the First Session of the Legislature, in the Year 1619* [13 vols.; Richmond, Va.: Printed by and for Samuel Pleasants, Junior, Printer to the Commonwealth, 1809–23], 4:475–78). Staunton was established as the seat of Augusta County in 1745; freeholders from Fincastle and Pittsylvania counties also published resolutions during the winter of 1775. Fincastle's Resolutions have received substantial analysis from historians (see Thad Tate, "The Fincastle Resolutions: Southwest Virginia's Commitment," *Journal of the Roanoke Valley Historical Society* 9, no. 2 [1975]: 19–31; Mary Kegley, "Who the 15 Signers Were," *Journal of the Roanoke Valley Historical Society* 9, no. 2 [1975]: 32–37; Jim Glanville, "The Fincastle Resolutions," *The Smithfield Review* 14 [2010]: 69–119; Mary Kegley, "Another Look at the Fincastle Resolutions," *Historical Society of Western Virginia Journal* 1 [2013]: 66–71).
4. The qualifications to be a freeholder and the likely meeting place in the town of Fincastle mean that many of the men came from the eastern part of Botetourt County, and their names can also be gleaned from among the court records of the period (*Virginia Gazette* [Dixon and Hunter], March 11, 1775, 3). In a statement of support and instruction to Virginia's representatives to the Continental Congress published two weeks later, Botetourt County's "freeholders and inhabitants" specifically noted that they "assembled at the courthouse" to compose their statement (see *Virginia Gazette* [Purdie], March 24, 1775, 3; *Virginia Gazette* [Pinkney], March 16, 1775, 2).
5. *Virginia Gazette* (Dixon and Hunter), March 11, 1775, 3; *Virginia Gazette* (Pinkney), March 16, 1775, 2.
6. *Virginia Gazette* (Dixon and Hunter), March 11, 1775, 3; Robert A. Gross, *The Minutemen and Their World* (New York: Hill and Wang, 1976), 47–50; T. H. Breen, *The Marketplace of Revolution: How Consumer Politics Shaped American Independence* (New York: Oxford University Press, 2004), 1–3.
7. *Virginia Gazette* (Pinkney), March 16, 1775, 2; *Virginia Gazette* (Dixon and Hunter), March 11, 1775, 3.
8. *Virginia Gazette* (Purdie), March 24, 1775, 3.
9. For specifics about Shenandoah Valley settlement practices, see Warren R. Hofstra's foundational work, *The Planting of New Virginia: Settlement and Landscape in the Shenandoah Valley* (Baltimore, Md.: Johns Hopkins University Press, 2004), 148–49, 197–218; Lyman Chalkley, *Chronicles of the Scotch-Irish Settlement in Virginia* (3 vols.; Rosslyn, Va.: The Commonwealth Printing Co., 1912–13), 1:177; and Rhys Isaac, *The Transformation of Virginia, 1740–1790* (Chapel Hill: University of North Carolina Press, 1982), 30, 90–91. For a listing of Botetourt County justices, see "Minutes of the County Court," in Lewis Preston Summers, ed., *Annals of Southwest Virginia, 1769–1800* (Abingdon, Va.: Lewis Preston Summers, 1929), 238–50; and H. R. McIlwaine, *Bulletin of the Virginia State Library* 14 (April/July 1921): 121–22, 126.

10. *Virginia Gazette* (Pinkney), March 16, 1775, 2; *Virginia Gazette* (Dixon and Hunter), March 11, 1775, 3. For a local history of Augusta County with a heavy focus on the Lewis family, see Joseph Addison Waddell, *Annals of Augusta County, Virginia, from 1726 to 1871* (1901; London, Eng.: Forgotten Books, 2012), 121, 126.
11. *Virginia Gazette* (Pinkney), March 16, 1775, 2; Waddell, *Annals of Augusta County*, 180, 127. Patrick Spero describes the trauma of frontier living in Pennsylvania during the eighteenth century, which was an experience comparable to that of the Virginia backcountry (see Spero, *Frontier Country: The Politics of War in Early Pennsylvania* [Philadelphia: University of Pennsylvania Press, 2016], 116–18).
12. "An Act for erecting two new Counties," in Hening, ed., *Statutes at Large*, 5:78–80. For a detailed overview of the settlement of the Shenandoah Valley, see Hofstra, *Planting of New Virginia*, 94–102; Turk McCleskey, *The Road to Black Ned's Forge: A Story of Race, Sex, and Trade on the Colonial American Frontier* (Charlottesville: University of Virginia Press, 2014), 1–9; David Hackett Fischer and James C. Kelly, *Bound Away: Virginia and the Westward Movement* (Charlottesville: University of Virginia Press, 2000), 111–26; Ann E. McCleary, "The Turnpike Towns," in Warren R. Hofstra and Karl Raitz, eds., *The Great Valley Road of Virginia: Shenandoah Landscapes from Prehistory to the Present* (Charlottesville: University of Virginia Press, 2010), 193–97.
13. Peter Silver notes that Indian war was especially frightening to rural European settlers because the battles and skirmishes did not feel like "proper violence" and did not follow European military strategy. In fact, Indian war "was designed by its practitioners to be precisely as terrifying as they found it" (see Silver, *Our Savage Neighbors: How Indian War Transformed Early America* [New York: W. W. Norton & Company, 2008], 56–57; Otis K. Rice, *The Allegheny Frontier: West Virginia Beginnings, 1730–1830* [Lexington: University Press of Kentucky, 1970], 40; Alan Taylor, *American Revolutions: A Continental History, 1750–1804* [New York: W. W. Norton & Company, 2016], 44).
14. *Virginia Gazette* (Hunter), September 19, 1755, 3. Draper's Meadow is on the present-day campus of Virginia Tech in Blacksburg, Virginia (see Waddell, *Annals of Augusta County*, 30; B. Scott Crawford, "A Frontier of Fear: Terrorism and Social Tension along Virginia's Western Waters, 1742–1775," *West Virginia History: A Journal of Regional Studies*, new series, 2 [2008]: 1–2). The governors of Maryland and Massachusetts discussed the attacks in their correspondence (see Horatio Sharpe to William Shirley, August 29, 1755, in *Correspondence of Governor Horatio Sharpe, 1753–1771* [4 vols.; Baltimore: Maryland Historical Society, 1895], 1:273).
15. Richard Middleton, *Pontiac's War: Its Causes, Course, and Consequences* (New York: Routledge, 2007), 61–64; Gregory Evans Dowd, *A Spirited Resistance: The North American Indian Struggle for Unity, 1745–1815* (Baltimore, Md.: Johns Hopkins University Press), 33–34; Colin G. Calloway, *The Shawnees and the War for America* (New York: Viking, 2007), 56–58; Ian K. Steele, *Setting all the Captives Free: Capture, Adjustment, and Recollection in Allegheny Country* (Montreal, Can.: McGill-Queen's University Press, 2013), 163–64; John Stuart, "Transcript of the Memoir of Indian Wars and other Occurrences, 1749–1780," Virginia Museum of History & Culture, Richmond, Va. For a full list of the women and children taken captive at Greenbrier, see William S. Ewing, "Indian Captives Released by Colonel Bouquet," *Western Pennsylvania Historical Magazine* 39 (1956): 195–96; Steele, *Setting all the Captives Free*, 439–551; Clarence S. Brigham, ed., *British Royal Proclamations Relating to America, 1603–1783* (12 vols.; Worcester, Mass.: American Antiquarian Society, 1820–1911), 12:212; Rice, *Allegheny Frontier*, 58–59; Griffin, *American Leviathan*, 21–22. Woody Holton argued that the 1768 treaties were ineffective at undoing the 1763 line, but he noted that settlement by backcountry individuals and families must be viewed separately from land speculators. Particularly in the "near backcountry" regions along the Greenbrier River Valley, 1769 marked a drastic increase in settlement (see Holton, "The Ohio Indians and the Coming of the American Revolution in Virginia," *Journal of Southern History* 60 [1994]: 453–55; and James Corbett David, *Dunmore's New World* [Charlottesville: University of Virginia Press, 2013], 56–62).
16. "An Act for Dividing the County

and Parish of Augusta," November 1769, in Hening, ed., *Statutes at Large*, 8:395–96, 398; *Virginia Gazette* (Purdie and Dixon), November 23, 1769, 3; *Virginia Gazette* (Rind), November 23, 1769, 2; Mary B. Kegley and F. B. Kegley, *Early Adventurers on the Western Waters* (5 vols.; Orange, Va.: Green Publishers, Inc., 1980–2004), 1:91; "Division Line between Augusta County and Botetourt County," June 13, 1770, Botetourt County Land Records.

17. "Act for Dividing the County and Parish of Augusta," Hening, ed., *Statutes at Large*, 8:398. The dividing line between Botetourt and Fincastle ran west from the Great Valley Road, roughly along U.S. 460 through present-day Christiansburg and Blacksburg, Virginia, and into present-day West Virginia along the New River and Kanawha River, before reaching the Ohio River, which the line followed to the south and west. The name "Fincastle" was chosen after Lord Dunmore's son, George Murray, Lord Fincastle. Fincastle County existed from 1772 to 1776, and after it was disbanded, the area was incorporated into several counties including a large portion that became Kentucky (see "An Act for Dividing the County of Botetourt into Two Distinct Counties," February 1772, in Hening, ed., *Statutes at Large*, 8:600; "Dividing Line between Botetourt County and Fincastle County," May 3, 1773, Botetourt County [Va.] Land Records, deed book 1, 1770–1773, Botetourt County Reel 1, LGRC, Library of Virginia, Richmond; and Christopher E. Hendricks, *The Backcountry Towns of Colonial Virginia* [Knoxville: University of Tennessee Press, 2006], 111).

18. The Greenbrier River Valley communities in the early 1770s, beginning in the north, included the "Little Levels" near present-day Hillsboro and Mill Point, West Virginia. Moving down the valley from the Little Levels along U.S. Route 219, the Spring Creek area included present-day Renick and Frankford and offered an abundance of relatively level land along the Greenbrier River and its offshoots. The "Levels," sometimes referred to as the "Big" or "Great" Levels, and occasionally combined with descriptions of the Spring Creek area, provided a counter to the Little Levels and encompassed the largest area of the Greenbrier Valley around present-day Lewisburg. To the east of the Levels, the mouths of Anthony Creek and Howard Creek moved from the Greenbrier River to their headwaters in the northeast near the present-day border between West Virginia and Virginia. Sinking Creek was to the west of the Levels and included several smaller valleys parallel to the larger section of the Greenbrier Valley, and Muddy Creek was to the southwest. The Greenbrier River cut across the Valley along the south side of Muddy Creek Mountain, and the communities to the south of that point were occasionally lumped together and described as the area "from the Influx of Mudie Creek down"; however, they included discrete communities along Wolf Creek, Indian Creek, and the "Sinkhole lands." The Sinkhole lands, also referred to as "the Sinks," are a geological phenomenon prevalent throughout the Greenbrier Valley because of the karst topography of the region.

19. David, *Dunmore's New World*, 76–83. In 1776, Fincastle County was renamed and divided into the counties of Montgomery, Washington, and Kentucky (Robert L. Scribner, Brent Tarter and William James Van Schreeven, eds., *Revolutionary Virginia: The Road to Independence* [7 vols.; Charlottesville: University Press of Virginia, 1973–83], 1:219–20).

20. "Appendix E," in Reuben Gold Thwaites and Louise Phelps Kellogg, eds., *Documentary History of Dunmore's War, 1774: Compiled from the Draper Manuscripts in the Library of the Wisconsin Historical Society and Published at the Charge of the Wisconsin Society of the Sons of the American Revolution* (cited hereafter as *Documentary History*) (Madison: Wisconsin Historical Society, 1905). The Lewises were originally from Augusta, but Andrew's home near present-day Salem, Virginia, was within the boundaries of the recently formed Botetourt County (established 1769). William Christian was the son of prominent Shenandoah Valley settler, Israel Christian. William Christian was brother-in-law to Fincastle's William Campbell, who had married another one of Patrick Henry's sisters. Christiansburg, Virginia, was named after William Christian in the 1850s (see ibid., 428–30; Scribner, Tarter, and Van Schreeven, eds., *Revolutionary Virginia*, 2:106). The "northern militia" consisted of men from Hampshire, Frederick, and Berkeley counties.

21. William Christian to William Preston, June 22, 1774, Draper Mss., 3QQ42, Microfilm, State Historical Society of Wisconsin, Madison. Stuart wrote that "[a]t the time we commenced our march no track or path was made" (see Stuart, "Transcript of the Memoir of Indian Wars"; Fleming, "Journal," *Documentary History*, 282; Joseph Johnson, Pension Record S31782, transcribed by C. Leon Harris, *Southern Campaigns Revolutionary War Pension Statements* [cited hereafter as SCRWPS]; John F. Winkler, *Point Pleasant, 1774: Prelude to the American Revolution* [Oxford, Eng.: Osprey Publishing, 2014], 49).

22. *Virginia Gazette* (Pinkney), November 10, 1774, 2. The style of fighting from behind trees and brush was particularly effective for the French and Indians fighting against General Braddock during the Seven Years' War and had been adopted by many frontier fighters. Historian John Grenier describes the eighteenth-century colonial frontier as the proving ground of this type of "petite guerre" strategy, which became America's "First Way of War" (see John Grenier, *The First Way of War: American Warmaking on the Frontier, 1607–1814* [Cambridge, Eng.: Cambridge University Press, 2005], 10–12; Isaac Shelby to John Shelby, October 16, 1774, in *Documentary History*, 276; William Fleming, "Orderly Book, Journal of the Expedition," in *Documentary History*, 343; J. F. D. Smyth, *A Tour in the United States of America: Containing an Account of the Present Situation of That Country . . .* [2 vols.; Dublin, Ire.: Price, Moncrieffe, 1784], 1:168–69). Numerous accounts describe the battle lasting a full day (see Samuel Gwinn, Pension Record S17992, transcribed by C. Leon Harris, SCRWPS; Samuel Vance, Pension Record S1882, transcribed by Will Graves, SCRWPS; George Doherty, Pension Record S1807, transcribed by Will Graves, SCRWPS). John Todd reported that the men collected spoils of war strewn about the battlefield, including "23 Guns 80 Blankets 27 Tomahawks with Match coats Skins Shout [shot] pouches pow[d]erhorns Warclubs &c. The Tomhawks guns & Shout pouches were sold & amounted to near 100" (see Fleming, "Orderly Book," *Documentary History*, 345–47).

23. *Virginia Gazette* (Purdie and Dixon), November 10, 1774, 4; William Christian to William Preston, October 15, 1774, in *Documentary History*, 265; William Fleming to William Bowyer, n.d., in *Documentary History*, 309; William Fleming to Nancy Fleming, n.d., in *Documentary History*, 253.

24. Fleming, "Orderly Book," in *Documentary History*, 348; William Christian to William Preston, October 15, 1774, box 1, reel 1, Campbell-Preston-Floyd Families Papers, Manuscript Division, Library of Congress, Washington, D.C.

25. Fleming, "Orderly Book," in *Documentary History*, 348. Dunmore was camped about fifty miles north of Point Pleasant near the present-day Hocking River (known as the "Hohocking River" in the eighteenth century) with 800 or 900 men (see Smyth, *Tour in the United States*, 1:162; Isaac Shelby to John Shelby, October 16, 1774, in *Documentary History*, 277; William Christian to William Preston, October 15, 1774, in *Documentary History*, 263; Joseph Hundly, Pension Record S5581, transcribed by C. Leon Harris, SCRWPS; Lord Dunmore to the Earl of Dartmouth, December 24, 1774, in *Documentary History*, 386; Virgil Anson Lewis, *History of the Battle of Point Pleasant Fought between White Men and Indians at the Mouth of the Great Kanawha River (now Point Pleasant, West Virginia) Monday, October 10th, 1774* [Charleston, W.Va.: The Tribune Printing Co., 1909], 56; Griffin, *American Leviathan*, 120; Joseph Doddridge, *Notes on the Settlement and Indian Wars of the Western Parts of Virginia and Pennsylvania from 1763 to 1783* [Akron, Ohio: New Werner Company, 1912], 177).

26. William Christian to William Preston, October 15, 1774, in *Documentary History*, 262. The numbers of dead and wounded vary, but contemporary reports are consistent in their approximation of fifty killed and eighty wounded, though later accounts by John Stuart, who fought in the battle, noted seventy-five killed and 140 wounded (see Fleming, "Orderly Book," in *Documentary History*, 344; *Virginia Gazette* [Purdie and Dixon], November 10, 1774, 4; Smyth, *Tour in the United States*, 1:169; Stuart, "Transcript of the Memoir of Indian wars"). For an explanation of other variations, see *Documentary History*, 344n65. Some of these men included James Curry, Alexander Stuart, and Alexander Walker (see Dunmore's War [Virginia Payrolls/Public

Service Claims, 1775], Microfilm; James Curry, Pension Record S44230, transcribed by C. Leon Harris, SCRWPS; Alexander Stuart, Pension Record VAS1817, transcribed by C. Leon Harris, SCRWPS; Alexander Walker, Pension Record R11040, transcribed by Will Graves, SCRWPS).

27. Lord Dunmore to the Earl of Dartmouth, December 24, 1774, in *Documentary History*, 371.

Chapter 3

1. J. F. D. Smyth, *A Tour in the United States of America: Containing an Account of the Present Situation of That Country . . .* (2 vols.; London, Eng.: G. Robinson, 1784), 2:65–68; Devereux Jarratt, *The Life of the Reverend Devereux Jarratt, Rector of Bath Parish, Dinwiddie County, Virginia* (Baltimore, Md.: Warner & Hanna, 1806), 14.
2. Jarratt, *Life of Devereux Jarratt*, 12–25, quotes from 13–15 and 24.
3. Philip Vickers Fithian, *Journal and Letters of Philip Vickers Fithian, 1773–1774: A Plantation Tutor of the Old Dominion* (Williamsburg, Va.: Colonial Williamsburg, 1943), 96 ("destroying"); Rhys Isaac, "'The Rage of Malice of the Old Serpent Devil': The Dissenters and the Making and Remaking of the Virginia Statute for Religious Freedom," in Merrill D. Peterson and Robert C. Vaughan, eds., *The Virginia Statute for Religious Freedom: Its Evolution and Consequences in American History* (New York: Cambridge University Press, 1988), 162; Jarratt, *Life of Devereux Jarratt*, 86; Janet Moore Lindman, "Acting the Manly Christian: White Evangelical Masculinity in Revolutionary Virginia," *William and Mary Quarterly*, 3rd ser., 57 (2000): 393–401.
4. Rhys Isaac, *The Transformation of Virginia, 1740–1790* (Chapel Hill: University of North Carolina Press, 1982), 192–93; John Ragosta, *Religious Freedom: Jefferson's Legacy, America's Creed* (Charlottesville: University of Virginia Press, 2013), 52–55.
5. Douglass Adair, "The Autobiography of the Reverend Devereux Jarratt, 1732–1763," *William and Mary Quarterly*, 3rd. ser., 9 (1952): 346–93; John E. Selby, *The Revolution in Virginia, 1775–1783* (Williamsburg, Va.: Colonial Williamsburg Foundation, 1988), 33; Jewel L. Spangler, *Virginians Reborn: Anglican Monopoly, Evangelical Dissent, and the Rise of the Baptists in the Late Eighteenth Century* (Charlottesville: University of Virginia Press, 2008), 36.
6. Jarratt, *Life of Devereux Jarratt*, 21–22, 84.
7. David Mossom et al., to the House of Burgesses, August 1751, in William Stevens Perry, ed., *Historical Collections Relating to the American Colonial Church* (2 vols.; 1870–78; New York: AMS Press, 1969), 1:382–83 ("Glory"), 384; Jonathan Boucher, *A View of the Causes and Consequences of the American Revolution; in Thirteen Discourses, Preached in North America Between the Years 1763 and 1775* (London, Eng.: G. G. and J. Robinson, 1797), 100–104; James Maury, *To Christians of Every Denomination Among Us, Especially Those of the Established Church* (Annapolis, Md.: Anne Catharine Green, 1771), 31–32.
8. Thomas E. Buckley, *Church and State in Revolutionary Virginia, 1776–1787* (Charlottesville: University Press of Virginia, 1977), 11; John K. Nelson, *A Blessed Company: Parishes, Parsons, and Parishioners in Anglican Virginia, 1690–1776* (Chapel Hill: University of North Carolina Press, 2001), 43–45, 48–56.
9. Isaac, *Transformation of Virginia*, 192–93; Paul K. Longmore, "'All Matters and Things Relating to Religion and Morality': The Virginia Burgesses' Committee for Religion, 1769 to 1775," *Journal of Church and State* 38 (1996): 778–81; Ragosta, *Religious Freedom*, 52–55.
10. Michael Grossberg, "Citizens and Families: A Jeffersonian Vision of Domestic Relations and Generational Change," in James Gilreath, ed., *Thomas Jefferson and the Education of a Citizen* (Washington, D.C.: Library of Congress, 1999), 17–20, 26; Gordon S. Wood, *Empire of Liberty: A History of the Early Republic, 1789–1815* (New York: Oxford University Press, 2009), 551–52.
11. Allan Kulikoff, *Tobacco and Slaves: The Development of Southern Cultures in the Chesapeake, 1680–1800* (Chapel Hill: University of North Carolina Press, 1986), 300–311; Jan Lewis, *The Pursuit of Happiness: Family and Values in Jefferson's Virginia* (New York: Cambridge University Press, 1983), 48–50.
12. Buckley, *Church and State*, ix, 30–36; Charles F. Irons, "Believing in America: Faith and Politics in Early National Virginia," *American Baptist Quarterly* 21 (2002): 397–407, William Woods quoted on page 404

("he knew"); Ragosta, *Religious Freedom*, 40–41, 58–70, 75; Spangler, *Virginians Reborn*, 197–200, 216–22, 229.

13. Buckley, *Church and State*, 17–18; Isaac, "Rage of Malice," 145–46; Jarratt, *Life of Devereux Jarratt*, 186–87; Virginia Bill of Rights quoted in Nelson, *Blessed Company*, 295; Ragosta, *Religious Freedom*, 59–61; Spangler, *Virginians Reborn*, 207.
14. Buckley, *Church and State*, 43; Charles F. Irons, "The Spiritual Fruits of Revolution: Disestablishment and the Rise of the Virginia Baptists," *Virginia Magazine of History and Biography* 109 (2001): 176–77; Jarratt, *Life of Devereux Jarratt*, 122, 123.
15. George MacLaren Brydon, *Virginia's Mother Church and the Political Conditions Under Which It Grew* (2 vols.; Philadelphia: Church Historical Society, 1947–52), 2:418–21, 426–27; Jarratt, *Life of Devereux Jarratt*, 186; Rev. Alexander Balmain quoted in Buckley, *Church and State*, 82.
16. John Buchanan quoted in George MacLaren Brydon, "David Griffith, 1742–1789: First Bishop Elect of Virginia," *Historical Magazine of the Protestant Episcopal Church* 9 (1940): 213–14; "A Member of the Established Church," *Virginia Gazette* (Purdie), November 1, 1776, 1; Buckley, *Church and State*, 84; H. J. Eckenrode, *Separation of Church and State in Virginia: A Study in the Development of the Revolution* (New York: Da Capo Press, 1971), 74–76, 84.
17. James Madison to Thomas Jefferson, July 3, 1784, in Julian Boyd et al., eds., *Papers of Thomas Jefferson* (43 vols.; Princeton, N.J.: Princeton University Press, 1950–), 7:360–61; Buckley, *Church and State*, 38–39, 56–61, 70–78, 86–87, 106–7; Eckenrode, *Separation*, 78–81; bill for a general assessment quoted in Jon Kukla, *Patrick Henry: Champion of Liberty* (New York: Simon & Schuster, 2017), 280.
18. Buckley, *Church and State*, 38–39, 90–91, 97–98, 109–10, 113; Eckenrode, *Separation*, 76–77, 83–89, 92–95, 97, 99–102, 107–8; John Blair Smith to James Madison, June 21, 1784, in William T. Hutchinson et al., eds., *The Papers of James Madison, Congressional Series* (17 vols.; Charlottesville: University Press of Virginia, 1962–), 8:80–83.
19. Buckley, *Church and State*, 144–49, 154; Eckenrode, *Separation*, 112–13; H. James Henderson, "Taxation and Political Culture: Massachusetts and Virginia, 1750–1800," *William and Mary Quarterly*, 3rd ser., 47 (1990): 104–5; Archibald Stuart to John Breckinridge, October 21, 1787, in John P. Kaminski et al., eds., *The Documentary History of the Ratification of the Constitution* (18 vols.; Madison: State Historical Society of Wisconsin, 1988), 8:89.
20. Buckley, *Church and State*, 161–69; Eckenrode, *Separation*, 118–29; Ragosta, *Religious Freedom*, 89–90.
21. Thomas E. Buckley, "Evangelicals Triumphant: The Baptists' Assault on the Virginia Glebes, 1786–1801," *William and Mary Quarterly*, 3rd. ser., 45 (1988): 33–40, Baptist petition quoted on page 56; Irons, "Spiritual Fruits," 173–74, 186.
22. Irons, "Spiritual Fruits," 173–74, 186; Buckley, "Evangelicals Triumphant," 42–44; Buckley, *Church and State*, 166; Eckenrode, *Separation*, 125–27, 135–36.
23. Brydon, *Virginia's Mother Church*, 2:493–97, 501–2; Buckley, "Evangelicals Triumphant," 40–56, law quoted on page 54; Eckenrode, *Separation*, 133–52.
24. Philip Norborne Nicholas quoted in *Richmond Enquirer*, May 26, 1804; Brydon, *Virginia's Mother Church*, 2:504; Eckenrode, *Separation*, 148–49, 501–2; David John Mays, *Edmund Pendleton, 1721–1803, A Biography* (Cambridge, Mass.: Harvard University Press, 1952), 341–45.
25. Brydon, *Virginia's Mother Church*, 2:452, 478; Buckley, "Evangelicals Triumphant," 66–67; John Marshall quoted in William Meade, *Old Churches, Ministers, and Families of Virginia* (2 vols.; Philadelphia: J. B. Lippincott Col, 1857), 1:30.
26. Richard Beale Davis, ed., *Jeffersonian America: Notes on the United States of America Collected in the Years 1805–6–7 and 11–12* (San Marino, Calif.: Huntington Library, 1954), 135; Meade, *Old Churches*, 1:301, 2:85; Isaac Weld, Jr., *Travels through the States of North America and the Provinces of Upper and Lower Canada, During the Years 1795, 1796, and 1797* (2 vols.; London, Eng.: John Stockdale, 1800), 1:177 ("with the windows").
27. Brydon, *Virginia's Mother Church*, 2:493; Thomas E. Buckley, "After Disestablishment: Thomas Jefferson's Wall of Separation in Antebellum Virginia," *Journal of Southern History* 61 (1995): 449; Buckley, "Evangelicals Triumphant," 55.
28. Henderson, "Taxation and Political Culture," 104–11.

29. Auguste Levasseur, *Lafayette in America in 1824 and 1825: Journal of a Voyage to the United States* (2 vols.; Philadelphia: Carey and Lea, and New York: White, Gallaher & White, 1829), 1:222–23; Annette Gordon-Reed, *The Hemingses of Monticello: An American Family* (New York: W. W. Norton, 2008), 641–45.
30. Brent Tarter, *The Grandees of Government: The Origins and Persistence of Undemocratic Politics in Virginia* (Charlottesville: University of Virginia Press, 2013).
31. Jarratt, *Life of Devereux Jarratt*, 15.

Chapter 4

1. Thomas Jefferson to William Gordon, July 16, 1788, in *Founders Online*, National Archives, https://founders.archives.gov/documents/Jefferson/01-13-02-0266 (accessed August 1, 2024); Declaration of Independence, July 4, 1776, *America's Founding Documents*, National Archives, https://www.archives.gov/founding-docs/declaration-transcript (accessed August 2, 2024); Patrick Henry, "Give Me Liberty or Give Me Death Speech," in William Wirt, *Sketches of the Life and Character of Patrick Henry* (New York: S. Andrus and Sons, 1849), 142.
2. A close reading of colonial runaway slave advertisements demonstrates how enslaved people challenged the traditional conventions of authorship and wrote themselves into history. For a fuller account, see Antonio T. Bly, "'Indubitable signs': Reading Silence as Text in New England Runaway Slave Advertisements," *Slavery and Abolition* 42 (2021): 240–68. For a powerful analysis of literacy as a signifier of civilization and history, see Henry Louis Gates, Jr., *The Signifying Monkey: A Theory of African-American Literary Criticism* (New York: Oxford University Press, 1988). In a letter addressed to Samson Occom, Phillis Wheatley documented the Black American desire to own themselves. Written shortly after she had earned her own freedom, the former slave-poet spoke in unaccustomed candor about the paradoxical nature of the American Revolution and the enslavement of persons of African descent:

    Rev'd and honor'd Sir,
    I have this Day received your obliging kind Epistle, and am greatly satisfied with your Reasons respecting the Negroes, and think highly reasonable what you offer in Vindication of their natural Rights: Those that invade them cannot be insensible that the divine Light is chasing away the thick Darkness which broods over the Land of Africa; and the Chaos which has reign'd so long, is converting into beautiful Order, and reveals more and more clearly, the glorious Dispensation of civil and religious Liberty, which are so inseparably Limited, that there is little or no Enjoyment of one Without the other: Otherwise, perhaps, the Israelites had been less solicitous for their Freedom from Egyptian slavery; I do not say they would have been contented without it, by no means, for in every human Breast, God has implanted a Principle, which we call Love of Freedom; it is impatient of Oppression, and pants for Deliverance; and by the Leave of our modern Egyptians I will assert, that the same Principle lives in us. God grant Deliverance in his own Way and Time, and get him honour upon all those whose Avarice impels them to countenance and help forward tile Calamities of their fellow Creatures. This I desire not for their Hurt, but to convince them of the strange Absurdity of their Conduct whose Words and Actions are so diametrically, opposite. How well the Cry for Liberty, and the reverse Disposition for the exercise of oppressive Power over others agree, I humbly think it does not require the Penetration of a Philosopher to determine. (*Connecticut Gazette*, March 11, 1774, 3).

3. Agency has become a recurring theme in the history of the Black experience in revolutionary Virginia. In Benjamin Quarles's "Lord Dunmore as Liberator," for example, enslaved Afro-Virginians answered the Governor's call to arms. In Sylvia R. Frey's study, Black Virginians emancipated themselves. In Woody Holton's *Forced Founders*, they emerged as pivotal actors in the events leading up to the colony's break with Great Britain. A thought-provoking reinterpretation of the revolutionary era in the Chesapeake, Holton's study uncovered what French intellectual historian, Pierre Nora, would describe as an important memory of the American Revolution. When threatened by the actions of the fictive members of their families, most of whom

were held in captivity, Thomas Jefferson, George Washington, William Byrd III, Landon Carter, and many Virginians of the gentry class sided with their contemporaries in other colonies in declaring independence. By demanding their own freedom, Black Virginians proved themselves not only founding fathers in their own right, but also powerful agents of history whose efforts to realize their own natural rights played a significant role in the political currents of the day. By revolting, they inspired their reluctant white counterparts to *truly* embrace the idea of revolution. In Noel B. Poirier's study of the Continental army, Afro-Virginians proved themselves "sable sons" of freedom who not only answered the British call to arms, but also expanded colonial notions of liberty by protesting the "peculiar institution" with their feet. Not long after the colony's Royal Governor established martial law, declaring "all indented Servants, Negroes, or others" free for their service to "His MAJESTY'S Crown and Government," the local leaders in Virginia were compelled to change their policy toward enlisting African Americans. Two years following Dunmore's infamous Proclamation, Poirier explained, the legislatures in the colony passed an act emancipating all enslaved Virginians, specifically those who would agree to serve in *their* militia units. In Philip D. Morgan and Michael L. Nichols's study of fugitive slaves in the Chesapeake, Virginians of African descent emerge as ardent champions of freedom's cause. Far from the idle characters shown in most histories of the American Revolution, they too experienced the contagion of liberty that spread throughout the colonies. Rather than wait for the Revolution, they ran. They demanded their freedom. They secured their sovereign rights over themselves. Most of these "sons of Ethiopia," Morgan and Nichols noted, did not wait to be invited into the fight. Far from it. Before the Royal Governor issued his decree, freeing all "slaves" who were willing to serve the Crown, before even their masters began contemplating their relationship with their kin on the other side of the Atlantic, Black Virginians fermented their own revolution, the ideological roots of which lay in the tragic story of their unique, racialized captivity. Over the course of the eighteenth century, they left, exercising their natural rights to their life and liberty. To them, freedom signified happiness. When the colonial conflict escalated, increasing numbers of enslaved Virginians seized upon the occasion to liberate themselves from the despotism of their former masters. While Cassandra Pybus's contemplation of the accuracy of Thomas Jefferson's estimation regarding these slave defections suggest that the Virginian planter overstated his case, her analysis nonetheless demonstrates that the Virginian slave owner was more than likely right on at least one thing in that regard. Mr. Jefferson's fears of an internal slave rebellion occurring during the burgeoning crisis were not misplaced. Enslaved Americans were actively engaged in the politics of the day. Slave flights were indeed increasing before the end of the era of the American Revolution. Many former slaves sided with the British. Some joined the ranks of the Patriots. Most, however, joined *Liberas*. Liberty, they declared loudly through their actions, was their preferred choice of master. In his *The Forgotten Fifth: African Americans in the Age of Revolution*, Gary B. Nash tells a similar story. Despite the uncertainty of the war, enslaved people fled bondage and offered their assistance to anyone who would dare to promise them their independence. Amid the Revolution, Black Virginians participated in what might have been the largest slave rebellion in early American history. As the founding fathers struggled to free themselves from the shackles of what they described as certain British tyranny, enslaved African Americans in the Chesapeake chose to do the same. Michael A. McDonnell's *The Politics of War* and, most recently, Judith L. Van Buskirk's *Standing in Their Own Light* also celebrated Black agency during the American Revolution. Virginians of color, they argued, proved active historical figures in their own life stories. Indirectly, they played an instrumental part in the unfolding events of the day. Passive they were not. As both McDonnell and Van Buskirk's studies reveal, they were deeply involved in the social, economic, and military issues of the age that inspired the grandiose but problematic language enshrined in the Declaration of Independence: that "all men are created equal" and further when it "becomes necessary for one people to dissolve the . . . bands which have connected them with another . . . Nature's God . . . requires" that they declare "the causes which impel them to the separation." And declare themselves independent they did, in ever increasing numbers (Benjamin Quarles, "Lord Dunmore as Liberator," *William and Mary Quarterly*, 3rd ser., 15 [1958]: 494–507; Sylvia R. Frey, "Between Slavery and Freedom: Virginia Blacks in the American Revolution," *Journal of Southern History* 49 [1983]: 375–98; Woody Holton, *Forced Founders: Indians, Debtors, Slaves and the Making of the American Revolution in Virginia* [Chapel Hill: University of North Carolina Press, 1999], 133–63; Woody Holton, *Liberty is Sweet: The Hidden History of the American Revolution* [New York: Simon & Schuster, 2021], 202–10; Pierre Nora, "Between Memory and History: Les Lieux de Mémoire," *Representations* 26 [1989]: 7–24; Noel B. Poirier, "A Legacy of Integration: The African American Citizen–Soldier and the Continental Army," *Army History* 56 [2002]: 20–23; Philip D. Morgan and Michael L. Nichols, "Slave Flight: Mount Vernon, Virginia, and the Wider Atlantic World," in Tamara Harvey and Greg O'Brien, eds., *George Washington's South* (Gainesville: University Press of Florida, 2004), 205; Lord Dunmore, Proclamation, November 7, 1775 [broadside]; Cassandra Pybus, "Jefferson's Faulty Math: The Question of Slave Defections in the American Revolution," *William and Mary Quarterly*, 3rd ser., 62 [2005]: 250–51; Gary B. Nash, *The Forgotten Fifth: African Americans in the Age of Revolution* [Cambridge, Mass.: Harvard University Press, 2006], 24–29; Michael A. McDonnell, *The Politics of War: Race, Class, and Conflict in Revolutionary Virginia* [Chapel Hill: University of North Carolina Press, 2007], 23–24; Judith L. Van Buskirk, *Standing in Their Own Light: African American Patriots in the American Revolution* [Norman: University of Oklahoma Press, 2018], 53–66; Declaration of Independence, July 4, 1776; Bernard Bailyn, *The Ideological Origins of the American Revolution* [Cambridge, Mass.: Belknap Press of Harvard University Press, 1992]).

4. *Virginia Gazette* (Purdie), December 12, 1777, 3. For insightful studies of advertisements for fugitives as a type of precursor to slave autobiographies, see David Waldstreicher, "Reading the Runaways: Self-Fashioning, Print Culture, and Confidence in Slavery in the Eighteenth-Century Mid-Atlantic," *William and Mary Quarterly*, 3rd ser., 56 (1999). 243–72. See also Bly, "Indubitable signs," 240–68.
5. *Virginia Gazette* (Purdie), December 12, 1777, 3; John J. Reardon, *Edmund Randolph: A Biography* (New York: Macmillan, 1974), 96–120.
6. Robert M. Randolph, *Peyton Randolph and Revolutionary Virginia* (Jefferson, N.C.: McFarland and Company, Inc., 2019), 11–13.
7. Ibid., 92–96, 122–28, 140–46, 164–67; Enclosure: Thomas Jefferson's Biography of Peyton Randolph (ca. 1723–75) [ca. July 26, 1816], *Founders Online*, https://founders.archives.gov/documents/Jefferson/03-10-02-0158-0002 (accessed August 2, 2024).
8. William Byrd II to the Earl of Orrery, July 5, 1726, in *Virginia Magazine of History and Biography* 32 (1924): 27. For a fuller account of the mindset of the eighteenth-century planter caste who imagined themselves as contemporaries of the Bible, see Anne Sorrell Dent, "God and Gentry: Public and Private Religion in Tidewater Virginia, 1607–1800" (Ph.D. diss., University of Kentucky, 2001); John K. Nelson, *A Blessed Company: Parishes, Parsons, and Parishioners in Anglican Virginia, 1690–1776* (Chapel Hill: University of North Carolina Press, 2001); and Anthony S. Parent, Jr., *Foul Means: The Formation of a Slave Society in Virginia, 1660–1740* (Chapel Hill: University of North Carolina Press, 2003).
9. Enclosure: Thomas Jefferson's Biography of Peyton Randolph.
10. *Virginia Gazette* (Purdie), December 12, 1777, 3; Julie Richter, "'The Speaker's' Men and Women: Randolph Slaves in Williamsburg," *Colonial Williamsburg Interpreter* 20 (2000): 47–51. For useful explications of personal servants, see William Roane's description of the responsibilities of his personal slave, Joe, in *Virginia Gazette* (Purdie and Dixon), August 17, 1769, 3; James Mercer's account of the duties of his personal slave, Christmas, *Virginia Gazette* (Purdie and Dixon), March 19, 1772, 3; Thomas Gaskins's advertisement for David, his personal slave, in *Virginia Gazette* (Purdie and Dixon), November 5, 1772, 3;

William Park's announcement concerning Peter, *Virginia Gazette* (Dixon and Hunter), December 19, 1777, 4; Charles Yates's discussion of Robin in *Virginia Gazette and Weekly Advertiser* (Nicolson and Prentis), September 20, 1783; John Breckinridge's report on Joe in *Virginia Gazette or American Advertiser* (Hayes), May 10, 1786; and John Fox's list of Gloucester's skills in *Virginia Independent Chronicle and General Advertiser* (Davis), July 28, 1790.

11. Edmund Randolph, "Essay on the Revolutionary History of Virginia, 1774–1782," *Virginia Magazine of History and Biography* 43 (1935): 216.
12. Richter, "'The Speaker's' Men and Women," 47–51; Continental Association, October 20, 1774, *Founders Online*, https://founders.archives.gov/documents/Jefferson/01-01-02-0094 (accessed August 2, 2024).
13. For the most comprehensive account of Virginia runaways, see the first volume (Virginia and North Carolina) of Lathan A. Windley's *Runaway Slave Advertisements: A Documentary History from 1730s to 1790* (Westport, Conn.: Greenwood Press, 1983). Interestingly enough, Johnny's invisibility is reinforced in the work of Peyton Randolph's most recent biographer, Robert M. Randolph.
14. Peyton Randolph, An Inventory of the Estate of Peyton Randolph taken January 5, 1776, in *Colonial Williamsburg Digital Library*, https://research.colonialwilliamsburg.org/DigitalLibrary/view/index.cfm?doc=Probates\PB00064.xml&highlight=peyton%20randolph (accessed August 2, 2024); *Virginia Gazette* (Purdie), December 12, 1777, 3; Linda Baumgarten, "'Clothes for the People': Slave Clothing in Early Virginia," *Journal of Early Southern Decorative Arts* 14 (1988): 40.
15. In John Trumbull's portrait of *George Washington* (1780), the artist documents the complex relationship between the general and his personal bondservant, Billy Lee (The Metropolitan Museum of Art, https://www.metmuseum.org/art/collection/search/12822 [accessed August 2, 2024]). Edward Savage's *The Washington Family* (1789–96) tells a similar story. In the center of that portrait of the Washingtons, the first president of the United States is shown at leisure with his wife, Martha, and her grandchildren. Off to the side of the painting, the artist included an enslaved man who most historians believe is Billy Lee, if not Christopher Sheels. Like the canvas done by Trumbull, Savage's painting captured the intimate relationship that existed between most enslavers and their personal slaves. The painting also arrests a scene most domestic slaves had little choice but to endure, that is pretending to be invisible in the presence of others (National Gallery of Art, https://www.nga.gov/collection/art-object-page.561.html [accessed August 2, 2024]). For useful analyses of eighteenth-century slave portraiture, the author consulted Agnes Lugo-Ortiz and Angela Rosenthal's *Slave Portraiture in the Atlantic World* (New York: Cambridge University Press, 2013) and Jennifer Van Horn's *The Power of Objects in Eighteenth-Century British America* (Chapel Hill: University of North Carolina Press, 2019).
16. As early as the seventeenth century, Virginia's burgesses broadcast written or printed documents orally. That practice continued into the eighteenth century. A passing search of the laws passed by the Virginia House of Burgesses highlights the complex relationship between orality and literacy in the tobacco colony. For several examples, see William Waller Hening, ed., *Statutes at Large; Being a Collection of All the Laws of Virginia from the First Session of the Legislature, in the Year 1619* (13 vols.; Richmond, Va.: Printed by and for Samuel Pleasants, Junior, Printer to the Commonwealth, 1809–23), 1:166 (1631), 1:341–42 (1647), 2:29–30 (1660), 2:108–9 (1661–62), 2:492–93 (1682), 3:442 (1705), 3:362 (1705), 3:512 (1710), 8:364–65 (1753). Studies by Gustafson and Isaac not only further highlight this, but also underscore communities wherein written and printed texts were performed (Sandra Gustafson, *Eloquence is Power: Oratory and Performance in Early America* [Chapel Hill: University of North Carolina Press, 2000], 1–33, 140–70; Rhys Isaac, *The Transformation of Virginia, 1740–1790* [Chapel Hill: University of North Carolina Press, 1999], 120–25). Throughout the American Revolution, slavery inspired the imaginations of the Founding Fathers. Like their New England cousins, Virginians also invoked the peculiar institution of racial slavery to describe the crisis between the colonial

and Great British. In 1769, for example, Peyton Randolph and his contemporaries exclaimed:

> We his Majesty's most dutiful Subjects, the late Representatives of all the Freeholders of the Colony of *Virginia*, avowing our inviolable and unshaken Fidelity and Loyalty to our most gracious Sovereign, our Affection for all our Fellow Subjects of *Great-Britain;* protesting against every Act or Thing, which may have the most distant Tendency to interrupt, or in any wise disturb his Majesty's Peace, and the good Order of his Government in this Colony, which we are resolved, at the Risque of our Lives and Fortune, to maintain and defend; but, at the same Time, being deeply affected with the Grievances and Distresses, with which his Majesty's *American* Subjects are oppressed, and dreading the Evils which threaten the Ruin of ourselves and our Posterity, by reducing us from a free and happy People to a wretched and miserable State of Slavery.

Levin Powell, who signed the Loudoun Resolves, used similar language. By his account, cosigned by his fellow Virginian, he proclaimed the imperial duties placed on the colony as "despotic exertion[s] of unconstitutional power designedly calculated to enslave a free and loyal people." Throughout the Revolution, early Americans described their relationship as one akin to bondage (Virginia Nonimportation Resolutions, May 17, 1769, *Founders Online*, https://founders.archives.gov/documents/Jefferson/01-01-02-0019 [accessed August 2, 2024]; "Public Meeting Loudoun in 1774," in James William Head, *History and Comprehensive Description of Loudoun County, Virginia* [Washington, D.C.: Park View Press, 1909], 128). For two comprehensive accounts of slavery in the imagination of America's revolutionary generations, see F. Nwabueze Okoye, "Chattel Slavery as the Nightmare of the American Revolutionaries," *William and Mary Quarterly*, 3rd ser., 37 (1980): 3–28; and Peter A. Dorsey, "To 'Corroborate Our Own Claims': Public Positioning and the Slavery Metaphor in Revolutionary America," *American Quarterly* 55 (2003): 353–86.

17. Rhys Isaac, "Preachers and Patriots: Popular Culture and the Revolution in Virginia," in Alfred F. Young, ed., *The American Revolution: Explorations in the History of America Radicalism* (DeKalb: Northern Illinois University Press, 1976), 125–56; Rhys Isaac, "Patrick Henry: Patriot or Preacher?" *Virginia Cavalcade* 31 (1982): 169–75; Thomas Jefferson to William Wirt, August 4, 1805, *Founders Online*, https://founders.archives.gov/documents/Jefferson/99-01-02-2187 (accessed August 2, 2024).
18. Gustafson, *Eloquence is Power*, 160–69; Isaac, *Transformation of Virginia*, 267–69. Incidentally, according to Julie Richter's study of the Randolph slaves, Eve and twelve other Randolph slaves ran away and joined the British sometime around 1781, a little over four years after John Harris left Edmund Randolph (Richter, "'The Speaker's' Men and Women," 49). As with Johnny, the Randolphs thought Eve a valuable piece of property. In Peyton Randolph's will, for example, the personal body servant of his wife was valued at £100, the same as his own personal servant (Randolph, Inventory of the Estate of Peyton Randolph). Eve's value is further documented in an advertisement that the Speaker's nephew, Harrison Randolph, had printed in James Hayes's *Virginia Gazette, or, American Advertiser* on February 2, 1782, shortly after the enslaved woman turned fugitive. Not long after her husband's death, Elizabeth (Betty) Randolph sold Eve to Harrison. Like Johnny, Eve was clearly aware of the political climate of her day. Before her flight, the British had occupied the city of Williamsburg, which in turn created an opportunity for the enslaved woman to declare her own independence:

    > TWENTY DOLLARS REWARD, For apprehending EVE, a Negro woman slave, who left York after the surrender; she is about forty years old, very black and slender, has a small mouth for a Negro, and a remarkable mole on her nose: She has since been seen on her way to Hampton. She carried with her a variety of striped and checked Virginia cloth cloathes. Whoever delivers her to the subscriber in Richmond, shall receive the above reward.

19. *Virginia Gazette* (Purdie), December 12, 1777, 3.
20. 1 Timothy 4:13 (King James Version). For a fuller account, see the third chapter of Antonio T. Bly, "Breaking with Tradition:

Slave Literacy in Early Virginia, 1680–1780" (Ph.D. diss., College of William & Mary, 2006).

21. James Blair, Bruton Parish to the Bishop of London, reel 12, p. 48, in The Fulham Papers, Lambeth Palace Library, London, Eng.
22. Antonio T. Bly, "'Reed through the Bybell': Slave Education in Early Virginia," *Book History* 16 (2023): 13–18; William Grimes, *Life of William Grimes, the Runaway Slave* (New York: n.p., 1825).
23. John C. Van Horne, ed., *Religious Philanthropy and Colonial Slavery: The American Correspondence of the Associates of Dr. Bray, 1717–1777* (Urbana: University of Illinois Press), 1–48.
24. A close reading of the published papers between the Associates of Dr. Bray and their counterparts in Virginia highlights not only an ethos of paternalism, but also an air of magnanimity, which explains, at least in part, why many slave-owning Virginians sent their slaves to the school.
25. [School Regulations,] September 30, 1762, in Van Horne, *Religious Philanthropy*, 190.
26. John Vogt, ed., *Register for the Bruton Parish, Virginia, 1662–1792* (Athens, Ga.: New Papyrus Publishing Company, 2004), 33, 35–36. For Randolph's slaves baptized as adults, see ibid., 28, 33, 35–36, 49, 53.
27. Antonio T. Bly, "In Pursuit of Letters: A History of the Bray Schools for Enslaved Children in Colonial Virginia," *History of Education Quarterly* 51 (2011): 429–59; Nelson, *Blessed Company*.
28. Thomas Jefferson to William Gordon, July 16, 1788, *Founders Online*, https://founders.archives.gov/documents/Jefferson/01-13-02-0266 (accessed August 2, 2024).
29. *Virginia Gazette* (Purdie), December 12, 1777, 3.
30. It was not usual for enslaved people to imitate the owner, all while developing their own unique sense of personhood. For a close reading of runaway slave advertisements and the ways in which the enslaved achieved resistance and agency, see Antonio T. Bly, "Pretty, Sassy, Cool: Slave Resistance, Agency, and Culture in Colonial New England," *New England Quarterly* 89 (2016): 457–92.
31. *Virginia Gazette* (Purdie), December 12, 1777, 3. Extant records suggest that John Harris might have secured his freedom in the age of the American Revolution. His name does not appear in any of the newspapers printed in America between 1777 and 1850. Nor does his name appear in any other records.
32. Michel-Rolph Trouillot, *Silencing the Past: Power and the Production of History* (1995; Boston: Beacon Press, 2015), 53; Nora, "Between Memory and History": 7–24. See also William H. McNeill, "Mythistory, or Truth, Myth, History, and Historians," *American Historical Review* 91 (1986): 1–10; Thomas Jefferson to William Gordon, July 16, 1788, *Founders Online*, https://founders.archives.gov/documents/Jefferson/01-13-02-0266 (accessed August 2, 2024).
33. R. G. Collingwood, *The Idea of History* (1946; Oxford, Eng.: Clarendon Press, 1993), 241.

Chapter 5

1. Colonel Joseph Reed to George Washington, December 22, 1776, *Founders Online*, National Archives, https://founders.archives.gov/documents/Washington/03-07-02-0324 (accessed August 9, 2024); George Washington to Lund Washington, August 20, 1775, *Founders Online*, https://founders.archives.gov/documents/Washington/03-01-02-0234 (accessed August 9, 2024).
2. Laurel Thatcher Ulrich, "Political Protest and the World of Goods," in Edward G. Gray and Jane Kamensky, eds., *The Oxford Handbook of the American Revolution* (online edition; New York: Oxford Academic, 2012). See also George Washington's direction that "Spinning should go forward with all possible dispatch, as we shall have nothing else to depend upon if these disputes continue another year" (George Washington to Lund Washington, August 20, 1775).
3. *Database of Virginia Military Dead*, Library of Virginia, https://www.lva.virginia.gov/public/guides/vmd/ (accessed August 9, 2024).
4. Bill for Dividing the County of Fincastle into Two Distinct Counties [October 15, 1776], *Founders Online*, https://founders.archives.gov/documents/Jefferson/01-01-02-0226-0002 (accessed August 9, 2024).
5. Jennifer L. Morgan, "*Partus Sequitur Ventrem*: Law, Race, and Reproduction in Colonial Slavery," *Small Axe* 22 (2018): 1–17.
6. Bond of Elizabeth Campbell and Jeremiah Smith, executors of William Campbell, September 27, 1781, Rockingham County Court.

7. Albert H. Tillson, Jr., *Gentry and Common Folk: Political Culture on a Virginia Frontier 1740–1789* (Lexington: University Press of Kentucky, 2014), 105.
8. "John Broddy/Broady," American Battlefield Trust, https://www.battlefields.org/learn/biographies/john-broddy (accessed August 9, 2024); David George Malgee, "A Frontier Biography: William Campbell of King's Mountain" (M.A. thesis, University of Richmond, 1983), 1,296.
9. Woody Holton, *Liberty is Sweet: The Hidden History of the American Revolution* (New York: Simon & Schuster, 2021), 202.
10. Graham Russell Gao Hodges and Alan Edward Brown, eds., *The Book of Negroes: African Americans in Exile after the American Revolution* (New York: Fordham University Press, 2021), xvii.
11. Cassandra Pybus, "Jefferson's Faulty Math: The Question of Slave Defections in the American Revolution," *William and Mary Quarterly*, 3rd ser., 62 (2005): 243–64.
12. "Robert Pleasants (1723–1801)," *Encyclopedia Virginia*, https://encyclopediavirginia.org/entries/pleasants-robert-1723-1801/ (accessed August 9, 2024); Robert Marsh application for revolutionary war pension file, National Archives Microfilm Publications.
13. Fallon Burner, "That's True Honor: Native American and Indigenous Veterans," https://www.colonialwilliamsburg.org/learn/deep-dives/thats-true-honor-native-american-and-indigenous-veterans/ (accessed August 9, 2024).
14. Lewis Preston Summers, *History of Southwest Virginia, 1746–1786: Washington County, 1777–1870* (Richmond, Va.: J. L. Hill Printing Company, 1903), 444.

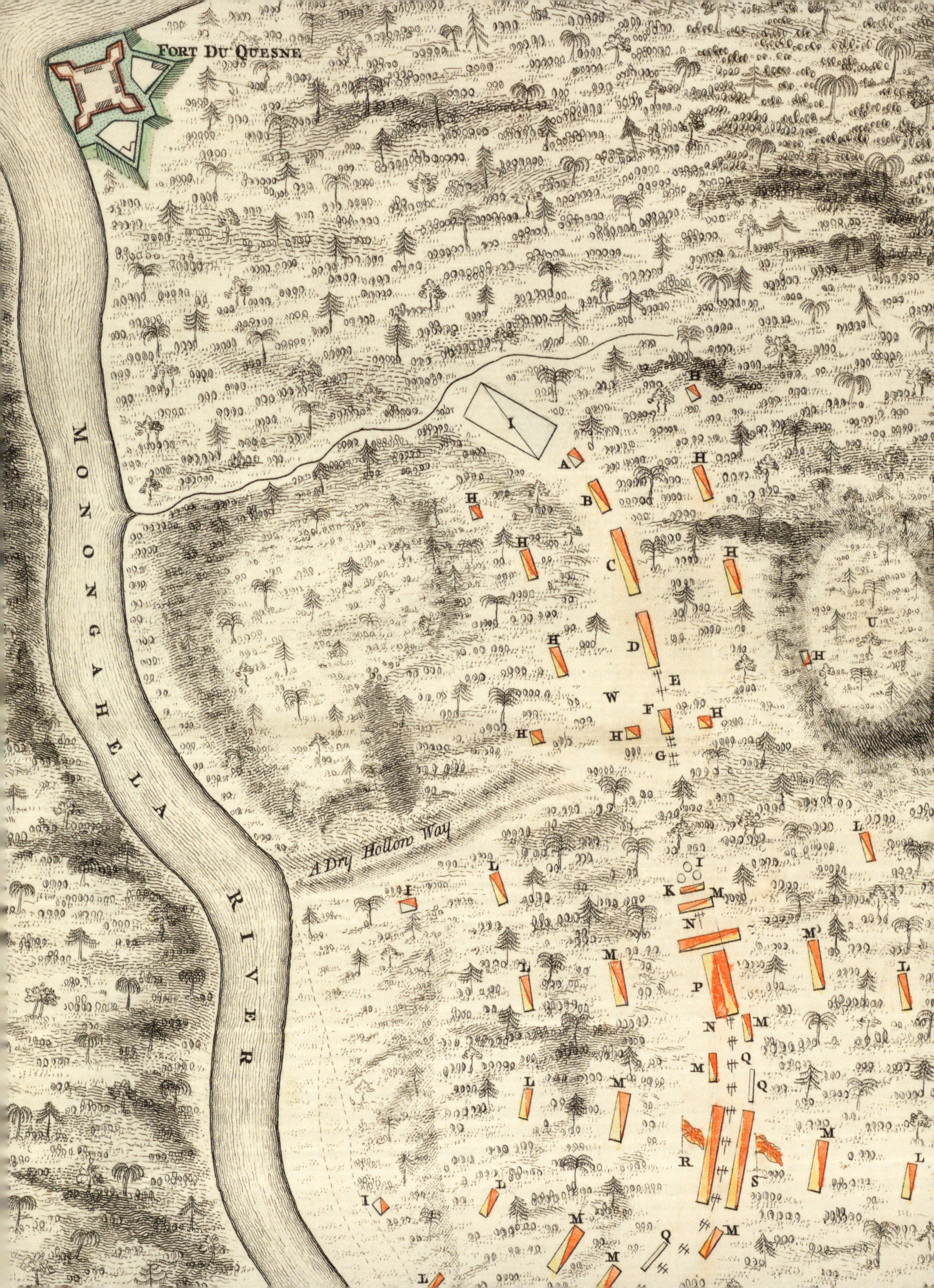

Fort Du Quesne
MONONGAHELA RIVER
A Dry Hollow Way

Index

Page numbers in *italics* refer to illustrations

Plans Showing the Braddock Expedition and Defeat in the Campaign Against Fort Duquesne, 1755 (detail), Robert Orme, 1758. VMHC, Bequest of Paul Mellon